CHRONICLES
FROM
THE EDGE

Kindest regards
from Norfolk.

Keith Skipper

CHRONICLES
FROM
THE EDGE

Keith Skipper

CHRONICLES FROM THE EDGE

Published in 2012

by:

Mousehold Press
Victoria Cottage
Constitution Opening
Norwich NR3 4BD

www.mousehold-press.co.uk

ISBN 978 1 874739 64 7

printed by Mimeo, Huntingdon

If a man loses pace with his companions, perhaps it is because he hears a different drummer. Let him step to the music which he hears, however measured, or far away.

Henry David Thoreau

Time will say nothing but I told you so,
Time only knows the price we have to pay;
If I could tell you I would let you know.

W.H. Auden

ACKNOWLEDGEMENTS

I am profoundly grateful to the *Eastern Daily Press*, the country's biggest-selling regional morning newspaper, for providing me with a regular parochial pulpit over the years.

Along with former editors Peter Franzen and Pete Waters, several other old friends and colleagues in Prospect House ensured my rushes of Norfolk enthusiasm could be calmed down and presented appealingly to all sections of a wide readership.

Warm thanks to Pete Kelley, Ian Bullock, Andy Russell, Trevor Heaton, Peter Hannam, Steve Snelling and a few more who drew short straws when the usual overseers were ploughing editorial furrows elsewhere.

Nods of appreciation too for Trevor Allen and a host of generous folk ready to decorate my words with telling illustrations. Mousehold Press publisher Adrian Bell again underlines his commitment to the Norfolk flag by finding this permanent home for my rants, raves and reflections.

My wife Diane and our sons Danny and Robin kept an eye on me during many safaris destined to yield articles and occasionally put forward alternative points of view to test an old man's rather biased stand on all matters Norfolk. I thank them now for adding valuable spice and perspective.

To all the rest who have inspired meaningful muses on my rounds in the shape of enlightening conversations and good-natured arguments, I offer the sort of handshake reserved for friends who know how to stir the Norfolk pot without forcing it to boil over.

Keith Skipper,
Cromer,
2012

INTRODUCTION

Living on the edge has been my lot since I first dabbled grass-stained toes in Beeston Lilypits and tempted post-war pollution into the open.

A village upbringing at the heart of agricultural Norfolk in years of austerity found me loitering with no intent on hazy headlands rather than digging in enthusiastically to impress the farmyard selectors. It looked too much like hard work out there among cattle, crops and weather-beaten critics of dilatory lads.

A seven-year grammar school detention in Swaffham fashioned mutual acceptance of a "dew diffrunt" mantra in the classroom. I decided to specialise from the age of 12 in the only two subjects for which I showed any aptitude, English and History. Mentors in other fields seemed happy enough to let me graze mostly on the outskirts of mainstream education.

Over three decades of full-time endeavour with local newspapers and radio left me tantalisingly short of that enclosure reserved for the media's top movers and shakers. Failure to grasp the basics of shorthand plus a lifelong fear of anything with knobs, switches and wires may have counted against me, along with lack of a driving licence, occasional lapses in deferential behaviour and a blunt refusal to pretend to be earnest about things that don't really matter.

As a soccer scribe, joyously elevated to covering Norwich City's varied fortunes under contrasting characters, hard-man Ron Saunders and flamboyant John Bond, I came to prefer the touchline of lonely independence to the dug-out of cosy subservience. Growing suspicions that the professional game might fall foul of ludicrous transfer fees and wages and cheap celebrity standards proved only too well founded.

As a weekday wireless operator, always reminding those listening in stereo I was the one "torkin' proper" in the middle, I gloried in the early freshness and freedom of a local BBC station allowed to use words like "indigenous", "parochial" and "squit".

For me, the "made in Norfolk" accumulator ran dry in 1995. I've been ploughing freelance furrows since as writer, broadcaster and entertainer. "Freelance" can mean existing on the periphery of just about anything, although it is a couple of steps up from "just resting" for actors and "contemplating my future" for redundant honeycart drivers and sugar beet knockers and toppers.

I have camped on the fringes of show business, not least as soulful lead vocalist with Captain Boyton's Benefit Band in the mid-1960s. The Norfolk Sound created by five press reporters is said to have reminded the Rolling Stones and Beatles not to take success for granted. Reckon that worked.

I strutted purposefully across the stage with Rackheath Players for several dramatic seasons blighted by a tendency to expect well-rehearsed colleagues to fall in with high-wire antics built on rampant ad-libbing. A cameo role as a Norfolk Compo in the early 1980s brought me down to earth in the company of hardened professionals presenting pantomime at Norwich Theatre Royal.

The chance to exchange banter with the redoubtable Nora Batty, that siren in curlers and pinafore from television's long-running Last of the Summer Wine, proved alluring enough to coax me towards proper respect for those who learn lines and know a cue when they hear one.

My role as leader of the travelling Press Gang entertainers – "antidote to Ant and Dec and the rest of Saturday night television" – underlined a need to stay true to local culture at a time when it could so easily be smothered by bland uniformity.

A mightily modest career as player with Caister Cricket Club saw me living meagrely on edges from an anxious crease, laughing at any batsman daft enough to miss one of my straight spinners and lingering in the outfield listening to the silence and dreading a steepler coming my way.

So where has all this flirting with the real things of life led me? Still living on the edge at Cromer next door to the Old German Ocean. (That's what I call the North Sea in order to attract an air of venerability in these image-conscious days).

Perhaps it's a perfect location for someone not quite sure of the best way to counter fears of Norfolk turning into everywhere else. Cromer may be a microcosm of a county trying to marry best of the old with least worrying of the new. Despite being a resident of Henry Blogg's domain for well over two decades, I'm none the wiser which shore we're pulling for.

That deep unease, occasionally spiced with bursts of anger, has characterised much of my writing in recent years although a precious Norfolk sense of humour continues to pull me back from the precipice of utter despair.

This selection of articles delivered from my regular *Eastern Daily Press* despatch box in various guises since the mid 1980s includes a fair amount of evidence to reinforce a reputation of someone who welcomes progress as long as it doesn't change anything. However, it also celebrates some of Norfolk's gloriously durable qualities, not least as displayed by colourful and life-enhancing characters met along the way and trend-resistant corners of the old empire where they tend to flourish.

Even the most ardent prophets of boom must recognise and respect these traditional virtues for what they are – true embodiments of the "dew diffrunt" mantra so many applaud while too few keep the faith.

As many of these articles carry a topical flavour, I give dates of their first appearances in one of the country's top provincial newspapers, a source of employment and inspiration for over half a century.

AFFORDABLE PLEA

November, 2010

Norfolk mawther Clare Dixon told the House of Commons a few home truths shortly before the clocks went back. I vote it already the most significant local battle-cry of the year. Trouble is I fear it will have little or no impact on a debate where forward thinking is as rare as silence on a train journey.

Clare travelled to London in late October to speak at a Westminster gathering as part of the National Housing Federation's Save Our Villages campaign, fighting for more affordable housing in rural areas. She stressed how she's been priced out of living in her childhood village by second-home owners and tourists.

The 29-year-old office manager rents a three-bedroom house with her boyfriend in North Creake but both would much prefer to live eight miles away in Brancaster, where they both grew up.

"Since I left my parents' home seven years ago I have moved six times around the area but have never lived in Brancaster – and that's where I want to be" said Clare. "A lot of houses there are holiday lets or belong to second-home owners. It's hard to find a private rented house at all, let alone an affordable one."

Clare's passionate plea, listened to with predictable nods of sympathy from MPs, councillors and special guests, reminded the government it's not just the unemployed and low income workers affected by a blatant lack of affordable housing.

Perhaps she's frightfully unlucky to feel such affinity for Brancaster, a fashionable fleshpot close to the golden cluster of Burnhams and a itself a leading member of the Coastal Colonisation Party dominated by well-heeled incomers ready and able to push out the boat in any choppy property seas.

Even so, someone desperate to drop anchor in pleasant waters where family roots already go deep ought to be allowed a sporting chance to go home and extend proud links. Never mind The Big Society. Let's hear it for The Real Community.

One of the most honest and succinct contributions to a long-running and complex debate came recently from blunt-talking Yorkshireman Paul Jackson, editor of *The Countryman* magazine, as he sized up the tide of change sweeping over village life;

"Fewer people work on the land. Pubs, shops, post offices and primary schools have closed. Public transport is non-existent or reduced to a trickle. Cottages have been taken over by wealthy second-home owners. Commuters have moved in while youngsters with a long line in ancestors from the area have moved out."

So do we have to embrace a new countryside for the 21st century? Are there too many groups and organisations fighting their own corners? Is the National Housing Federation a reasonable judge of what's really needed to keep rural areas alive? Are second-home owners chiefly responsible for killing our villages? What about the impact of glossy property programmes on television selling the rustic dream?

Regular strands in a complicated tapestry we can't expect to become any easier to unravel during an economic depression ... although it should be obvious that unless the countryside gets a more balanced population rather than just commuters, countless more pubs, shops and other facilities will go.

Here's another question to which we await a useful answer – what is "affordable" housing? I doubt prices are the same in North Norfolk as in the Cotswolds, West Cornwall or North-West Scotland. There's also the vital matter of jobs being available close enough to prevent new "affordable" housing occupants turning into instant commuters.

Nor should we underestimate strength of opposition in most small communities to building new houses of any kind. This topic stood out at every parish and rural district council meeting I attended as a young reporter at the heart of Norfolk in the early 1960s. I gather agendas headed "defending local character" still come first.

I suspect the second-home part of this saga has become too deeply mired in class warfare to attract much meaningful light. The general assumption seems to be that toffs, mainly from London, need a pretty and quiet bolthole to count their money before going back to pile up a bit more in the big city.

They are shadowy and elusive figures on the fringes of a vain battle to keep old-fashioned community virtues intact. They don't muck in and even refuse to pick up handy local dialect expressions at village hall bingo sessions.... like "Cor, blarst me, thass the fust house I're won this week!"

We do know many holiday homes sit empty for up to nine months of the year in North Norfolk's more desirable spots. Such a waste. And it must be true that in at least one good-looking coastal parish they've decided to change local Homewatch signs for Awaywatch stickers.

Good luck, Clare, and all with genuine desire to stay close and true to what they know and love. Priceless aims in an increasingly rootless and money-riven world.

Salthouse – part of the North Norfolk coastal 'colony'

ALWAYS FRESH

February, 2012

I'm often asked for my favourite Norfolk yarns and reasons why they have lasted so long.

See, an automatic assumption that I am ancient while our highly individual sense of humour, a potent mixture of squit, wit and shifty tales doused in dialect, is little more than an affectionate nod towards a gentler, slower age.

Perhaps the disappearance of so many good ole boys from cosy corners of our local pubs and a dramatic decline in numbers working on the land have cut off vital fresh supplies of earthy fun to the Norfolk Laughter Grid.

No doubt a grubby tide of stand-up spite and confrontational capers masquerading as entertainment has washed away most grounds for belief in a television service bent on provoking healthy laughter.

Comedian Vic Reeves, clearly pining for the good old days of Morecambe and Wise, Tommy Cooper, The Two Ronnies and Les Dawson, lamented recently; "Comedy has become very bitter. It's got quite nasty, quite venomous." Some will suggest he could have left "quite" out of that timely little script.

It's all very well claiming our comedy has to reflect hard times, question entrenched attitudes and force us to face up to difficult truths. But that begs no excuse for embarrassingly large rations of cruelty and crudeness, not even towards greedy bankers, blinkered politicians and football managers who must know their stupid or inflammatory words will be taken as gospel by so many.

Humour employed properly can diffuse messy situations, cut through cant and hypocrisy and throw a gentle light on scary dark corners. Humour ought to make us smile and think, not wince, worry and rant.

Wholesome Norfolk squit, with its stunning use of understatement, may have its roots in days when folk had to provide their own amusement or go without. Even so, I sense it could yet play an important role in our emergence from economic and spiritual depression.

From whence springs such new-dawn optimism? Well, I have witnessed enough revivals built on old-fashioned virtues and homely chuckles to appreciate anew sentiments expressed by rural writer Clarence Henry Warren about 70 years ago.

He mused; "It is one of the most attractive features of country humour that it never quite loses its freshness. It may be passed on from generation to generation but it remains a coin whose mintage is never dulled with use.

"The same may be said of country expressions which are not necessarily humorous at all –metaphors and likenesses and odd phrases which, once coined, have never gone out of currency."

He recalled a couple of his father's sayings; "It doesn't take long to do a five-minute job." And to anyone out and about unusually early in the morning; "You must have got up before you went anywhere."

Old boys in my home village would have added how often it picks a wet day to rain, how it gets late earlier when the clocks go back and how often they knocked a hole in the wall so they could dip their bread in next door's gravy.

I'm still collecting nuggets on my Norfolk rounds, more like little pebbles of whimsy dropped into oceans of debate about incinerators, wind turbines, council cuts, car parking charges and people who move to Norfolk and can only see a joke by appointment.

There's the one about Charlie showing a party of tourists round Great Yarmouth. He pointed out the very spot where Lord Nelson supposedly threw a gold sovereign across the River Yare. "That is impossible," snapped one of the visitors. "No-one could throw coins that distance."

"Ah, but yew hev ter remember," explained Charlie, "money went a rare lot farther in them days."

This one reached me via a regular source of material pounding the mean streets of Cromer. It features two venerable local characters watching a hearse rolling slowly by. As it disappeared into the distance, one inquired: "Who died, then?"

"Him in the box, I reckon," said the other.

"Yis," pondered the first, "driver looked orryte."

A Norfolk vicar dropped this on my collection plate. During his talk to the children, the young curate asked, "What is grey, has a bushy tail and gathers nuts in the autumn?"

Little Horry at the back raised his hand. "I know th'arnser orter be Jesus – but that dew sound wholly like a squirrel ter me."

Right, as you've read this far, I offer as a reward a couple from my Top 10. The others are on the way to BBC Television's Head of Light Entertainment.

Martha's husband died and she went to put an announcement in the local paper. She wanted to keep it as short as possible. "Jist put 'Billy Grimble dead'," she suggested. The girl told her she could have six words for the same price.

"Right," said Martha. "Kin yew add 'Ferret for sale.'"

Finally, Jacob and Eliza were relaxing in front of the fire as anniversary cards trembled on the mantelpiece above. The old gal turned to her husband of 70 years and asked: "Bor, if I should go afore yew, will yew promise me if yew tearke on sumwun else yew wunt let har wear my clothes?"

"Dunt yew fret, my bewty, cors I wunt," replied Jacob.

"Ennyway, they wunt fit."

BIBLE IN DIALECT

December, 2011

Novelist Anthony Trollope, no stranger to these parts in Victorian times when he worked as a Post Office Surveyor, declared to the nation: "There is, perhaps, no greater hardship at present inflicted on mankind in civilised and free countries than the necessity of listening to sermons."

Perhaps he sampled a few yawn-inducing marathons on his Norfolk rounds while searching for handy material to weave into the next best - seller. Pity he never savoured my village chapel diet of three sessions on a Sunday plus Tuesday Fellowship if cricket or homework didn't get in the way.

I can call up a host of colourful characters and memorable sermons. For instance, Harry Dawson, our Sunday school superintendent and local preacher with a simple but warmingly effective style, roused me from a summer afternoon reverie as he made reference to a recent funeral in the locality.

"Mr Littleproud may be the undertaker – but Jesus is the uppertaker!" You don't forget lines like that. It came bouncing back over the years as I heard of the death at 82 of the Rev. Colin Riches, a Methodist minister who not only maintained the Devil shouldn't have all the best tunes but also insisted he ought not to be allowed a monopoly on laughter and good yarns.

Colin had already assumed "divine" status in my eyes and ears by the time we joined forces in an attempt to lift religion above the almost-apologetic "God Slot" formality on Radio Norfolk's Dinnertime Show in the 1980s. Church and chapel chuckles became essential ingredients of our homely deliberations.

He shared extracts from familiar Bible stories first given a Norfolk coat of paint for Anglia Television's epilogue programme. This led to publication of *Dew Yew Lissun Hare*, a collection of New Testament favourites, and *Orl Bewtiful an New*, a similar tribute to the Old Testament.

He also broadcast dialect stories in Anglia's Highway programme and in BBC Television's Songs of Praise from the legendary Christmas show at Thursford.

I asked Colin what had influenced him to use our vernacular in this way. "Well, hearing Bernard Miles telling Bible stories on the radio in his delightful Hertfordshire accent set me wondering whether it would be possible to do the same thing in our not dissimilar Norfolk accent.

"Then there was Sidney Grapes. Having been minister for eight years in the Martham Circuit, which includes his native village of Potter Heigham, I found the idea more and more attractive." Time for Boy Colin to step out alongside Boy John and bring a new dimension to pulpit offerings.

Colin's dialect treatment leans delightfully on memories of old Methodist lay preachers lighting up sermons with homely parables of their own. My favourite comes from Colin's version of the Creation where God proved beyond doubt he can speak with a clear Norfolk voice - "Le's hev some loight on the job."

These Riches revisions have served me well in travelling productions like All Preachers Great and Small for local churches. Many Bible stories slip almost naturally into the Norfolk style, happily without running the risk of sounding irreverent.

He also gave me permission to feature a couple in my latest book, *Come Yew On, Tergether!* an anthology of Norfolk dialect writing. Cyril Jolly, long-serving Methodist preacher from Gressenhall, is also there – and in many ways he prepared the way for me to appreciate the Norfolk style of Colin Riches.

Cyril told how many years ago at Wendling Chapel the preacher noticed two women in the back row talking together during the singing of a hymn. He held up both hands and stopped the singing abruptly. In the silence, one of the women was heard to say: "Yis – and I allus fry mine in lard."

There can be no better tribute to Colin Riches than to recall the occasion when he made time stand still. In fact, it not only stood still – it went backwards.

He was holding forth on a glorious afternoon at Thurne. "There on the wall, facing the preacher when he stood in the pulpit was the innocent clock, there in the right position for the preacher to watch it. And that clock told me it was half-past two, so the service began.

"Thereafter, a miracle occurred. The service went so providentially well that at the close the hands of that innocent clock pointed to twenty-past one!

"You can imagine my ecstasy. If miracles like this were going to happen often, word would get around and perhaps I would for the big-time.... The steward came to the door with me. What he said brought me firmly down to earth. 'That ow clock up thare ...thass acted the fewl before. Suffun come adrift inside on it, and that go backards. Sorry abow that.'

"When I got home, I looked over my order of service for that afternoon. I chuckled to myself when I looked at the last hymn we had sung. It was Number 7 in the old Methodist hymnbook. The last line reads ... 'For ever and ever, when time is no more.'"

Colin Richards – leaning delightfully on memories of old Methodist lay preachers

BLOODSHOT CELERY

May, 2011

Methodist lay preachers of the old Norfolk circuit could trim country pulpits with homely sermons built on philosophical gems like: "The Lord, he knew what he wus a'dewin', mearkin' rhubarb come afore strawberries."

I have long regarded both as first-class seasonal treats and savoured this year's double bonus as they arrived early to set taste buds and childhood recollections working overtime. For all my ineptitude along the growing and picking fronts, I have cultivated deep respect and gratitude for creative creeds of others. Better than being eaten up with envy.

That shameless compromise began when father and useful members of his gardening corps banished me to dark corners of the shed to find a tray of King Edward seed potatoes wedged between a pile of old rubber boots and the green pram that took me and several others on early state visits round the village. I found a rat and a perfect excuse to rush indoors for a quiet read.

Although the foreman may have smelt a rat whenever I came up with a new excuse for missing digging, planting, watering, weeding and harvesting duties, it was generally agreed that my absence was far more likely to enhance productivity than develop the plot.

Adventures along strawberry rows in nearby parishes did lead to useful pocket money and vital contributions towards a blazer for the new school year ... although aversions to bopping below hedge level, concentrating beyond five minutes and putting my fragile back into anything more strenuous than Test Matches on the orchard pitch marked out between apple trees called for a few short cuts towards five bob.

I did a deal with several headscarved women whose flying fingers put my irritable fumbling to shame. They paid me a small fee to take their loaded baskets to the weighing and paying station. So I plodded instead of picked, mused rather than moaned, ate as many as possible without feeling too sick to travel and went home with just about enough money to warrant packed sandwiches and a bottle of cold tea for the next day's exertions.

Our home-grown rhubarb enjoyed an enviable reputation among neighbours always ready to barter with produce from their own fertile patches. I like to think I played a small but significant part in father's glow as tributes were paid and exchanges made. His bucket-and-spade sessions after visits to the outside family seat clearly boosted the quality of our generously-leafed quota. It was a proud team effort.

There lingered a tendency among a few also-rans in the rhubarb stakes to dismiss it as "no more than celery gone bloodshot" while its healthy purging qualities could be reduced to the poetic Norfolk chant of "drawing one's backside up to one's elbows". That is the sanitised version for those of a tender disposition.

I still prefer it neat, stewed with a drizzle of sugar, although I have been tempted into adding the odd downpour of evaporated milk for a Sunday tea diversion. Crumbles, pies and tarts are never turned away while rhubarb merged with other fruits can produce an outstanding variety of jams. Don't forget to add root ginger or pectin where necessary.

For all its obvious virtues, there remains a jokey flavour about one of my favourite treats. While replenishing stocks at a local outlet the other day, a broad Norfolk voice put my entire life's work and culinary tastes into perspective; "Yew talk it. Yew write it. Spooz yew might as well eat it anorl!" I took this completion of a hat-trick as a bit of a compliment.

Of course, the very word "rhubarb" is often used by actors talking quietly to one another on stage to simulate real conversation since it contains no harsh-sounding consonants and is hard to detect. Perhaps some of our elected representatives ought to follow suit when it comes to dispensing verbal fruit in parish council chamber or the House of Commons.

While rhubarb is normally considered to be a vegetable, a New York court decided in 1947 that since it was used in the United States as a fruit it should be counted as a fruit for the purposes of regulations and duties. One of the side effects was a reduction in taxes paid.

The United Kingdom's first rhubarb of the year is harvested by candlelight in dark sheds dotted around the noted "Rhubarb Triangle" of Wakefield, Leeds and Morley, a practice that produces a sweeter, more tender stalk. Wonder if estate agents put it in their brochures like this ... "Clear out the old and find regular joy in the new on this sought-after patch."

Used for medical purposes by the Chinese for thousands of years, the plant has grown wild along the banks of the River Volga for centuries. The cost of transportation across Asia made rhubarb very expensive in medieval Europe.

Rhubarb can be forced or encouraged to grow by raising the local temperature, usually by placing an upturned bucket over the new shoots. There we are, another sound use for the good old family pail. Even I could have managed that little cover-up operation.

BUCOLIC BUCCANEER

May, 2012

The file in my head marked "Outstanding Norfolk Characters" has long held a cherished place for marshman Eric Edwards, not least for the way he turned so many good friends into ardent admirers.

His recent death at 71 may have cast a temporary shadow over murmuring reed beds of the Norfolk Broads but that ruddy-faced smile and swishing scythe pinned to a backcloth that could have been ordered by Constable or Turner will live long and bright in countless memories.

We went back a tidy way. Some of Eric's tackles on local football pitches made me wince. I was a cub reporter on the touchline. "Hard but fair" and "tigerish wing-half" were lifted regularly from soccer's volume of handy clichés to describe this farmworker's no-nonsense approach to Saturday afternoon chores in the early 1960s.

Once, when the muse found an unlikely resting place on my shivering shoulder, I called him a "bucolic buccaneer". Eric won his county colours as a half-back along with the admiration of opponents, colleagues and spectators who knew an honest competitor when they saw one.

We met again over 30 years later when I put away my pen and picked up a scythe at Eric's chuckling invitation. Perhaps the bucolic buccaneer had a mean streak after all...

Employed by the Broads Authority since 1967 to manage reed beds and grazing marshes, he retained remarkable enthusiasm for someone whose art as one of the last hand-working cutters could soon be as obsolete as a half-back on the modern football pitch.

Before answering Eric's call to join him on a cutting safari I consulted the apprentices' handbook compiled in 1885 by Ernest Suffling. This description in *The Land of the Broads* might easily have been penned on the morning I tried my hand at one of Broadland's oldest crafts.

"During any open weather that may occur after Christmas, reed cutting is commenced and continued until the work is completed in early spring. It is, in fact, carried on until the sap begins to rise and young shoots are just appearing.

"In cutting an upward stroke is made with the sickle, the reed being held in bunches by the left hand, and care is taken to cut the reed as far below water as possible as a saying prevails that an inch of reed below water is worth two above it.

"This may be accounted for from the fact that the green part below the water turns, when dry, to a rusty black, becomes as hard as horn, and is consequently much more durable when placed upon the roof of a house in the form of thatch, with only these hard 'butts' exposed to the weather.

"When the boat is properly loaded it is propelled by a long pole called a quant to a landing place or staithe and the reed carefully landed."

My mentor chuckled. "You can't learn this from a book. Only from being on the marsh". A windmill stood guard under a bold blue sky as he coaxed me knee-deep into the water. I made a brave attempt to scythe and lay the reeds but had to borrow from Eric's row to thump on a drouncing board.

"Comb out all the rubbish and tie 'em up if they're dry enough" he instructed. "I told you mowing was hard graft... come and have a rest in my shed" smiled this natural communicator who enlightened hundreds of visiting schoolchildren each year. His shed was an instant museum it had taken him 30 years to create.

We clambered over rat traps, coypu catchers and wire sparrow cages to reach a collection of tools used over a century before. The crome was employed to drag plants out of the dyke. A didle scooped up the mud. Inevitably, he came back to the scythe, caressing it like an old friend. Leather reed cutters' thigh boots glowed with pride.

"They were soled in 1911" confided Eric. "About the same time as your first football boots," I suggested.

He was visited in his natural workplace by Prince Charles, Margaret Thatcher and Harry Secombe. He appeared on television's Generation Game to demonstrate reed-cutting skills. He was a splendid ambassador for the Broads Authority at a time of great change and challenge.

His MBE in 2004 drew widespread applause with one supporter suggesting it could stand for Master of the Broadland Empire.

On the day he saw little point in taking me on as an apprentice, Eric did offer the kind of reflections worthy of a new page in my Norfolk characters' file. Here they are as I watch him plying his trade among the bearded tits, moorhens and swaying reeds at How Hill nature reserve by the River Ant at Ludham:

"I love chatting to people about the magic of this place. Some say I work in a natural paradise and so I am insulated from changes going on in Norfolk and the rest of the world.

"But I see it simply as my job to carry on and do my little bit here. I want to leave something of interest and value for the next generation. Places like this will become even more important as life goes faster and we yearn for the gentler pace of old ways and old days."

Marshman Eric Edwards passing on a few tips to a dubious apprentice in the reed beds of the Broads

BUMPER CROP

November, 2008

As a regular passenger on the Trans-Norfolk Highway – well, the good bit that runs from Cromer to Hunstanton – I relish special offers at this time of year.

Geese arrow over moody marshes as breezes stiffen. Rusty leaves leap up and whirl round village war memorials decked out in new crimson. Turned-up collars are back in fashion on the coastal catwalk. The old game of "spot the local" is much easier to play.

Our mooch to Sunny Hunny on the back of icy blasts, cheerful interludes and earnest pledges to leave festive shopping for at least another month took an exciting diversion. We bought apples from the estate shop at Sandringham to stock up for winter.

Crumbles and pies by royal appointment, but I'll still drown them in gallons of evaporated milk. Some experts advise me this is an act of culinary treason punishable by increased girth and extra washing up. I say it's a matter of refined personal taste and private behaviour. On the other hand, how some people advertise tasty items for sale is a cause for widespread public concern.

Tiny chalky caterpillars are still being encouraged to crawl all over fruit and vegetables, be they wonky, curly or downright handsome. Another bumper crop of roadside apostrophes, along with a rash of dreadful spellings, is turning a traditional way of earning a few extra bob on the path to the great-season-of-too-much into a campaign for a swift return of the three Rs – Radish, Rhubarb and Red beet.

Some lazy abbreviations are bad enough – it was years before someone told me PYO didn't stand for Pickle Your Onions – but now those dratted caterpillars are nibbling into cabb's and pot's by the acre after summer feasting on straw's, rasp's, tom's and lett's. They also had a go at choc ice's, afternoon tea's and coach partie's.

We must put a full stop to the unwanted apostrophe and misspelling for the sake of our beleaguered education system and travellers on the Trans-Norfolk Highway with time to size up passing attractions. Drastic, I know, and probably illegal under the Human Rites (Growing Stuff) Act, but the only answer is the boycott of all transgressors.

Let me start the ball rolling on a positive note. I spotted only two correct versions of "potatoes" on our round trip of about 100 miles, so I hope certain roadside advertisers at Heacham and Holme enjoy healthy sales. The others might consider changing to "spuds" – without the apostrophe – and attending evening classes so they might avoid potential disasters like "autumn bizarre", "pubic meeting" and "bowels club outing".

There is a theory that some howlers pinned to parish notice boards and elsewhere are deliberate ploys to set tongues wagging and so spread the word more widely than usual. If that's the case, they're letting the subtle side down in Brancaster, Morston and Blakeney.

I looked in vain for "lithe muscles" to suggest Charles Atlas is flourishing in these well-heeled fleshpots where keeping fit has been known to involve a hectic dash round the second-home circuit.

Now that brings me neatly to another important topic of the hour, a powerful drive for peaceful coexistence between native, newcomer, weary weekender, fleeting tripper and ever-active opportunist exploiter. The Norfolk Independence Party's latest consultation paper, Cum Yew On, Tergether, calls for common ground to fertilise with straightforward regulations.

It is hard to argue with proposals to abolish the soulless A140, to tricolate the tricky A47 with more eco-tea stalls and to cobble the A11 before the recession is over. Slightly more contentious could be plans to offer rewards for staying put and radiating satisfaction with the same place for a long while.

The general idea is to treble payment of council tax for second homes but offer handsome concessions for faithful residents who have lived in the same house or immediate area for 30 years or more. A clear incentive to foster fresh community spirit before Chelsea-on-Sea spreads beyond Choseley.

Another key pointer to a brighter tomorrow is a suggestion that all those seeking the honour of representing Norfolk at Westminster should reside for a minimum of five years in the constituency they want to send them there. Similar rules are being sought with regard to parish, district and county council elections.

Finally, telling advice from this far-reaching document: "There's no better way of currying favour with Norfolk people than to accept they are different from the start and praise them openly for it instead of criticising behind their backs."

CAPITAL FUN

March, 2009

This is the heartwarming saga of a Norfolk woman who gave a freshly-minted pensioner a break – and then took bold steps to entertain him.

My wife's penchant for surprises blossomed like a springtime garden as I reached my 65th birthday. She plotted a path to a capital show based on one of my favourite books and films while also ensuring our sons would be there to lead the applause.

I should have sensed something special in the air as we set out for London on a bright Friday the 13th. We left the Bittern Line at Norwich where the Vicar of Cromer, the Rev David Court, headed for home after his capital excursion. "Still busy up there," he confided.

"We met on a Friday the 13th," I reminded my travel organiser and social secretary. Our hotel was but a villain's footfall from Portland Place, celebrated starting point for the ripping yarn about to dominate our weekend doings.

I can't quite match the master, Alfred Hitchcock, when it comes to building tension. I suspect you may have guessed already that *The 39 Steps* must now forever feature in my anecdotage.

This firm family favourite on screen and in print has been cheerfully adapted for the stage by Patrick Barlow and is still receiving rave notices at the Criterion Theatre. A cast of only four do wonders with John Buchan's fast-moving adventure while staying remarkably faithful to the Hitchcock black-and-white gem of 1935.

There have been two other full-screen versions since, starring Kenneth More and Robert Powell, plus a television "revival" a few months ago. Good judges like me, however, have no trouble in voting smooth Robert Donat the best Richard Hannay by far on celluloid.

Perhaps much of Buchan's original story penned in 1915 was lost in translation to the cinema but he had the good grace to regard the Hitchcock production as "a better story than my own".

Buchan died in 1940, just after completing five and a half years as Governor General of Canada. Earlier occupations included journalist, politician, diplomat, director of a publishing house and barrister. He wrote racily in his spare time and became as famous as any modern celebrity. His own son learned of his father's death not directly, but by spotting the news on newspaper posters in the street.

I couldn't help drawing the odd comparison between the brilliant Buchan and some current "personalities" while traipsing round Madame Tussaud's place on Sunday afternoon. Without pushing a pensioner's cussed streak to fresh heights, I had to ask elder son who certain people were and what they had done to demand my attention.

I posed happily with Lord Nelson, Charles Dickens, Albert Einstein, Henry VIII, Shirley Bassey and a few others popping up from my scrapbook of time. I enjoyed a taxi ride at the end to celebrate the history of a throbbing city which continues both to fascinate and intimidate me.

There appear to be more giant building sites than during our family safari last summer, cladding and scaffolding fingering the skies and clout-and-clang vying with traffic's chug-and-charge below. More hard hats than mobile phones in some places... now there's a novelty.

I recall this sort of teeming world opening my eyes and ears but hardening my heart against big-city life on my very first visit in the early 1960s. I kept wondering then how many people would have to drop dead on the pavement before anyone took any notice.

"I could never live or work here" ... hardly a surprise verdict to share with wife and lads. Still, we were here for the weekend all in my honour. I was duty bound to show a measure of appreciation.

Even Richard Hannay felt bored in London before all those spiffing escapades sent him to Scotland for a few dollops more, a gentleman adventurer on the run handcuffed to a woman of variable moods. Perhaps I was better off than I realised.

On the train journey home, passing the emerging Olympic dream at Stratford – now there's a useful setting for a modern Hannay to take on international odds – our conductor kept broadcasting reminders ... "don't forget to take your personal longings with you."

That line, which I may well have imagined, followed me all the way back to Cromer where daffodils danced in glorious fresh air.

I took at least 39 steps just to make sure the pier was still there.

TASTE TEST

A customer in the bakery shop asked the Norfolk girl who was helping if she ever ate the cakes.
"Blarst, no," she replied. "That'd be stealin'. I jist lick 'em!"

June, 2002

CITIZEN KANINE

February, 2009

It's surprising where your mind can wander on a quiet February afternoon in front of the fire. I like to think this is how outstanding works of culture flare into life.

A tailpiece on the news got me going. Owners and their pets had been treated to a special "paws in proceedings" at a cinema in Leiston showing Bolt, the latest Disney animation film with a doggy flavour.

Every conceivable pun was collared to give the bulletin a shiny coat – why on earth didn't they make it the lead item? – before a weather forecast bound to put walkies in cold storage for a day or two.

I yelped with envy as one shameless owner unleashed his parting shot about coming back next week "to see Citizen Kanine". That was all the licence I needed to go panting in search of pedigree chums.

He started it, I told my conscience, as Gundog Millionaire, The Hound of the Basketmeals and Corgi and Bess came sniffing round the corner. Time then to cock a leg a few rungs higher up the artistic ladder.

I resisted an obvious temptation to usher William Shuckspeare onto stage alongside my old actor friend, the late, lamented Peter Whitbread, who gave the Bard a distinctive Norfolk flavour during his memorable years with my Press Gang entertainers.

One of the highlights of his extensive repertoire aiming to prove Will really hailed from Stratton-on-Strawless was a scene from The Two Gentlemen of Verona. Peter stepped out as Launce, the clownish servant, with his dog Jack taking the part of Crab, to whom "the most scene-stealing non-speaking role in the canon" has been attributed. Jack invariably stole the show, cowering under his master's critical tongue and then turning doleful eyes towards an engrossed audience.

Hardly surprising as Jack took a bow-wow that a few more juicy Shakespearean roles should be tossed his way. We lined up Collieuranus, Mutt Fido About Nothing and Julius Seize'er! for starters.

Nor did it take a classic scholar to work out how Lady Macbeth dismissed the family hound each night before preparing her devoted husband's cocoa and mead... "Out, dammed Spot, out I say!"

Peter helped me make a start on completely rewriting the works of Shakespeare in broad Norfolk, an exercise launched on a wave of local versions of well-known titles.

For example, The Pedlar of Swaffham replaces The Merchant of Venice, Good Larf Full O'Mistearkes takes over from The Comedy of Errors and Bit Dark Over Will's Mother's is a natural Norfolk successor to The Tempest.

Many favourite quotations simply ask for the proper treatment. Turn to Richard III for "A dickey! A dickey! My kingdom for a dickey, ole partner!" and to Romeo and Juliet for "Cheerio, ole bewty. That ryte upset me ter see yew go, but I'll be abowt fust thing in th'mornin'."

Major challenges remain – there's little scope for troshing in Troilus and Cressida while Hamlet's appetite for squit is open to question – but a completion date of 2016 to coincide with the 400th anniversary of Shakespeare's death seems a reasonable target.

Remember, some of this began as a fireside reverie. It used to be common to peer into flames to see pictures. I tend to hear words lighting up countless little alleys to yesterday's desk in the village classroom.

We used to recite multiplication tables – a boy next to me knew the tune but often forgot the words – and prepare for regular spelling tests. We sorted out differences between rain, rein and reign, pour, poor and paw and rough, bough, ruff and bow.

There were catchy rhymes and silly sentences to help the teaching process. I still know that "preface" stands for Peter Roberts Eating Fish, Arthur Catching Eels while "contents" reminds me Cows Ought Not To Eat Nasty Turnip Stalks.

My wife recalls colours of the rainbow through the line Roy Of York Gave Battle In Vain, first letter of each word representing Red, Orange, Yellow, Green, Blue, Indigo and Violet.

With such vital memory tools in place, I don't resent a few hours of enforced hibernation before spring rings its welcoming bell.

Another path beckons after all that barking business with dogs at the pictures. Where did I pick up that wonderful line about a miserable woman who could only see a joke by appointment?

Probably Alan Bennett. Wonder if he ever tried to give Timon of Athens a broad Yorkshire accent...

CITY MUSINGS

November, 2011

The last drops of daylight were being squeezed out of a grumpy November sky as I waved to a cheery market stallholder and joined other upwardly mobile folk in The Forum.

Is it really 10 years since this futuristic giant landed to lord it over the city, question so many traditional tastes in architecture and strive to live without embarrassment next door to the glorious St Peter Mancroft Church?

Perhaps it is a measure of the way this bustling meeting place has settled into a generally accepted Norwich picture that some early opponents find it hard to believe as much time has fled to cover any tufts of doubt left sprouting above the market place.

My lingering reservations mainly concern finding enough window cleaners with heads for heights and sufficient opportunities to read a full chapter before being lured into another bout of people-twigging. Honestly, I prefer my nose in a book to poking it into someone else's business.

Forum forays cannot match railway trips for being forced to share bits of other people's lives and longings, especially when the simple art of communication descends into technological babble, but it takes a stronger will than mine to totally ignore a constantly changing floor show full of colour, movement and intrigue.

I am drawn easily to outrageous fashions and mannerisms of the young and bewildered looks on faces of the elderly who have run out of coffee and chat and can only sit and wonder what the world is coming to. An obvious generation gulf – but rarely a threatening cloud hanging over it. It is a big place in which it can be just as easy to ponder as to pronounce.

Most of my city safaris include a Forum interlude to savour a page or three of a freshly-acquired book, hopefully with enough appeal to salve my conscience for adding yet another to groaning shelves and to prevent too much people-twigging.

My latest purchase may add up to immediate reward for taking domestic duties seriously enough to visit a cathedral exhibition of beautifully-designed tea towels. All Washed Up (now there's a good name for an autobiography) bowls along in the Hostry until November 26.

A customary loiter in Elm Hill induced a smart idea for a board game in which you try to cover as many cobbles as possible with autumn leaves to soften the going. I had just thrown a six when a broad Norfolk voice from the other side called out "What are yer lorst, boy? Ent no crabs down here!"

Time to rediscover my social equilibrium in the wonderful world of books. I glanced at bargain "left-overs" lined up outside the shop like wallflowers at a 1950s school dance. It soon became evident that such tantalising imagery was not entirely wasted on my one-pound choice, *Literary Lapses* by Stephen Leacock.

The name rang a bell.... a school bell from an end-of-term treat in 1957. An English master with a grander sense of humour than the rest of the staff put together read us a couple of essays by "this Canadian teacher who hated teaching but decided it should be fun all the same." He laughed longer and louder than us, possibly out of acceptance he had too much in common with Mr Leacock.

I did note one line in my exercise book for possible use in any exam where hyperbole might be encouraged –"Lord Ronald flung himself upon his horse and rode madly off in all directions." Sadly, no opportunity arose to employ such frantic activity and I lost contact with its daring creator.

Suddenly, more than half-a-century after that classroom treat wasted on too many of us, I am ready for any number of lessons in laughter with the man once hailed as the most popular humorist in the English-speaking world.

Stephen Leacock moved to Canada at the age of six with his family from Hampshire, England, and carved out an international reputation as a comic writer. It was said in 1911 that more people had heard of him than had heard of Canada,

He died in March, 1944, just a few days after I was born. Literary Lapses, first published in 1910, is a treasury of his talents and a sharp reminder of what I've been missing all these years.

Take his version of boarding-house geometry: "The landlady of a boarding-house is a parallelogram – that is, an oblong, angular figure which cannot be described but which is equal to anything. A wrangle is the disinclination for each other of two boarders that meet together but are not in the same line."

Or the world of insurance: "Now, I detest life-insurance agents. They always argue that I shall some day die, which is not so. I have been insured a great many times, for about a month at a time, but have had no luck with it at all."

I took my Leacock discovery to The Forum for a few more sips of culture. I suspect the watcher became the watched for once as that funny old chap over there with his nose in a book keeps laughing out loud and slapping his thighs.

CONCRETE CARPET

July, 2011

This summer marks the 25th anniversary of one of the most significant "whither Norfolk?" arguments in my lifetime. It brokered a new spirit of honesty between diehards manning the drawbridge and missionaries preaching the gospel of progress and prosperity.

Yes, a quarter of a century has raced past, even by the occasionally sluggish standards of Nelson's county, since one of our parliamentary representatives launched the Great Debate on how far and how fast we could go without surrendering ignominiously to commuters, congestion and convulsions brought on by artificial expansion fired by short-term thinking and the fast-buck philosophy.

Loaded slightly in favour of more sensitive souls, perhaps, but my reading of John MacGregor's famous "carpet of concrete" speech in 1986 was based largely on relief that at last someone important had found the courage to speak out and a belief he really wanted fresh thinking on matters previously dismissed as off limits. Like priceless meadows being sacrificed, not because the natives needed houses so much as strangers were demanding dormitories.

The South Norfolk MP, then Chief Secretary to the Treasury, went on to become a key figure in the Thatcher and Major governments hardly remembered for dipping green fingers into an embattled countryside. He was made a life peer as Baron MacGregor of Pulham Market in July, 2001. An accomplished magician, he should be lauded even now for attempting the mighty difficult trick of stirring the Norfolk pot while following a strict Westminster menu.

His stark warning of how an increasingly popular place to live and work could turn into "a dormitory sprawl on a carpet of concrete" collected big headlines but scant support among his fellow Conservative MPs in Norfolk. Yarmouth's Michael Cartiss said it was far too early to talk about concrete jungles. Ralph Howell (North Norfolk) called for a warm welcome for those wanted to live here. "We have a lot of space and we don't need to worry about too much development yet." Henry Bellingham, still going strong in North-West Norfolk, suggested that high unemployment meant the county could no longer afford "to say it wants to stay as it is."

At least Sir Paul Hawkins, The Tories' father figure in South-West Norfolk, chipped in with a pertinent observation to widen discussions: "I believe there has been for some 15 to 20 years far too much haphazard development going hand in hand with poorly designed houses. Look at almost any village or small market town and see pleasant older centres surrounded by bungalow growth."

That thread was picked up and woven into a passionate argument against creeping urbanisation by historian Correlli Barnett, who coined the term "The Middlesex Look" in the early 1970s to describe modern housing development in rural Norfolk. He moved here from Surrey.

"When I go back to the Home Counties it seems every road is congested and every village has become a mini-suburb. It's possible that through continued growth of population and industry, Norfolk might acquire what is defined as increased prosperity – but it will have lost something we greatly value. Perhaps those of us who have come from other parts of the country can see this more clearly because we value the difference.

"If you live in a fine castle with lovely grounds and there's a vast horde coming towards you, why not draw the bridge up? If people in East Anglia wish to protect their way of life and fear the consequences of great change, why not? Norfolk exists as a complete living environment for the people who are here. It does not exist as a facility for the rest of the country."

I cherish those sentiments from a gifted "incomer" prepared to accept the most alluring of gravy trains could demand a series of tracks carving through the richest pastures, the prettiest corners, the quietest backwaters and the most cherished landscape. It was no wonder the parochial spirit emerged so strongly at times of so much imposed change.

The MacGregor salvo inspired several other influential voices to echo his warning. Norfolk Naturalists' Trust director Moira Warland, another comparative newcomer, pointed out dangers to precious habitats through intensive agriculture and increasing flocks of visitors drawn to a beautiful countryside. The Norfolk branch of the Country Landowners' Association claimed the policy of concentrating development in larger villages would produce huge satellites to the detriment of small communities. Outspoken county councillor John Birkbeck laid into the tourism bandwagon as well as excessive development.

Five summers later, the county's High Sheriff, Thomas Cook, made a scathing attack on "fly-by-night developers ruining the place, an insidious enemy which masquerades under the name of economic development." The growth lobby urged him to get his head out of the clouds.

No doubt similar advice will be offered to those with the audacity to make a fuss when current expansion ideas, especially around Norwich, start turning into concrete reality. It will be too late then to ring the Pulham Market consultancy set up to shed a little light on murky subjects long before "localism" promised a lot more than it is likely to deliver.

RIGHT LINE

Ian Emmerson, who died recently at 82, set me up for one of the neatest ad-libs of my career. The man who made such a consistently bold mark as director at Norwich's Maddermarket Theatre gave me a lengthy interview on his retirement in 1989.

I concluded our chat on BBC Radio Norfolk with the obvious question about what he might do now to relax.

"Well, the garden could do with a bit of attention," he replied.

"Ah," I mused, "the plot thickens....."

His broad smile and nod of approval hinted I had found the right line for the occasion.

February, 2007

CURTAIN CALLS

March, 2011

Sharing a dressing room with Olly Day on a moonlit Saturday night at the end of Cromer Pier ought to be compulsory treatment for anyone who has lost contact with the sunny side of the street. His irrepressible humour and optimism are perfect signposts to renewed joy in simply being part of the Great Norfolk Variety Show.

Olly's stage menu of magic, mirth and music has earned him a tidy living and strong following for over 20 years along with his role as entertaining road safety ambassador in local schools. An obvious appeal to all ages sets him apart as talented all-rounder rooted in old-fashioned virtues.

I've known and liked him long enough to appreciate theatrical flair is a genuine extension of a homely and engaging personality as caring family man and dependable friend. The fact he can live up to such billing without putting on airs and graces or bending the knee to showbiz shenanigans suggests a host of hearty curtain calls to come.

Our reunion at the Pavilion Theatre as he hosted a successful fundraising show in aid of arts projects at the new Cromer hospital revived memories of a milestone occasion on the pier in the summer of 1984. A Night of Squit, featuring homespun performers who had become firm favourites on the local wireless, launched a quarter of a century of travelling entertainment.

My troupe of followers, gradually evolving into the Press Gang as demands increased and fixtures multiplied, matured together to form a mean green machine recycling the sort of material which used to fill village meeting places before television ruled so many lives.

We returned to the end of Cromer Pier in 2008 to give thanks for such uplifting diversions and to pay homage to Dick Condon, our Irish inspiration, for realising that squit was as good as blarney when it came to putting bums on seats.

Olly, mixing magic tricks and well-loved songs with fast-emerging confidence built on natural cheekiness, played his part in underlining the strength of parochial entertainment on that 1984 line-up. A burgeoning solo career took a handy stride forward.

Perhaps a smile-in-your-face style could be curtailed somewhat by use-your-imagination demands of radio, but his flights of fancy from Larks End and other exotic places certainly intrigued many listeners.

I can vouch for a highly unorthodox approach to more "serious" topics when we teamed up now and again to present the Dinnertime Show on BBC Radio Norfolk. It remains a matter for conjecture to this day as to who was supposed to be setting an example worthy of Lord Reith's legacy.

We welcomed as a guest Sir Alfred Jules Ayer, better known as A J Ayer, or "Freddie" to his friends, a renowned philosopher noted for his promotion of logical positivism. He was doing the rounds to promote his latest book about Thomas Paine, Thetford's most famous son.

I nudged Olly towards *Rights of Man, Common Sense* and *Age of Reason*, Paine's highly influential political writings of the 18th century, and urged him to brush up on the French Revolution and American War of Independence. I would concentrate on Professor Ayer's reputation as a fine cricketer and supporter of Tottenham Hotspur FC.

As the great man was ushered in for this twin assault on fundamental beliefs and sporting preferences, my good-natured colleague rose from his seat, proffered a welcoming hand and extended a cordial greeting: "Hello, old cock. What do you do?"

Sir Alfred Jules Ayer said he was a writer and philosopher. "What, you sit and philosophise and then write about it?" was Olly's follow-up icebreaker. By the time we went live on air they were like old chums who'd just met up in the pub by chance while I tried to remember if he was a batsman or bowler.

Such a refreshing coming together of bright if contrasting minds found uncanny echoes when I brokered a pre-Radio 2 arts show exchange between playwright Arnold Wesker and lateral thinker Sid Kipper, modest megastar from St Just-near-Trunch. He combines singing, storytelling, broadcasting and writing in seamless fashion although some can fall foul of his sideways stance.

The man who wrote *Roots* to place Norfolk on an international stage at first seemed wary of so potent a blend of squit and culture as Sid stepped away from normal thought processes and explored unlikely avenues for fresh inspiration. He was just being himself. An hour or so later his new-found friend and admirer was roaring with laughter and jotting down Kipper gems for future reference.

Olly Day – talented all-rounder rooted in old-fashioned virtues

DIALECT DREAMS

May, 2010

Even a seasoned and curmudgeonly old stick-in-the-mud like me can appreciate an occasional dip into fresh streams of thought. A man at the top of our road invited a veritable plunge with his casual inquiry: "Do you dream in dialect?"

Now, he might have been hinting at a mildly obsessive streak following me around for the best part of half-a-century as writer, broadcaster and entertainer in my native Norfolk. It's easy now to get a bit of a reputation when you preface erudite observations with "Cor, blarst me!" or "Thass a rum ole dew!"

Perhaps he sees me as some kind of bucolic visionary ready to lead lost souls into a new linguistic sunlight. Or as a dangerous fundamentalist refusing to accept that days are numbered for mardling mawthers and fair-ter-middlin' mawkins.

Whatever his motive behind that amiable inquisition over the garden wall, it stirred me into bursts of deep reflection throughout a run of events soaked in local culture.

I certainly hear echoes of another Norfolk, another age, in my dreams, a time and place where buttercups and blackberries blot out bedraggled suburbs and ugly by-passes.

Yes, the accent's on nostalgia, and I suppose we can influence our own slumbering pictures to some extent, but any voices raised from the past seem to call for honest comparisons.

As most of those voices chided and challenged me along snakes-and-ladders country lanes and across cows-or-crops fields, they must carry a coating of Norfolk dialect.

I take it for granted that a good old boy dropping in to make sense of a highly complex dream set in Norfolk would interpret being wise after the event as "wunt a'went if I'd a'known". And he'd point to knockin' and toppin', back-breaking lot of sugar beet workers before mechanisation, as the perfect scene to counter romantic notions about toil on the land.

Maybe some of his nocturnal musings had been coloured by the work of Mary Mann, a farmer's wife who produced superbly-crafted stories packed with acute feeling for rich dialect and ruined lives. She was determined to highlight rural plight rather than rustic charm.

I selected this gritty chronicler of our Victorian countryside to launch a series about local writers on my monthly visit to BBC Radio Norfolk for a Tuesday teatime mardle. Mary Mann (1848 – 1929) deserves to be hailed as this area's answer to Thomas Hardy.

While many suggest we could do much better than St George as our patron saint, I reckon it's handy to have a full day of homely introspection rather than blustering jingoism. I settled for a gentle Norfolk song of praise.

An invitation to present a "patriotic programme" on April 23 to help Norwich Blackfriars Rotary Club's charities at home and abroad gave me the ideal excuse to extol our precious character and emphasise the need to preserve it.

The annual uplifting celebration of our still-vibrant vernacular attracted the usual full house to Cromer Parish Hall. This time Friends Of Norfolk Dialect accepted a much higher profile than before as festival offerings and party pieces rang out defiantly.

There was also an exceptionally hearty reception for a non-competitor from Sheringham – Cromer largesse can reach heartwarming levels – as Peter Brooks received honorary life membership of the organisation set up in 1999.

Peter followed me as Fond chairman and has earned the mantle of elder statesman through his wise and measured approach to various posts and countless little difficulties. All those years in local government taught him the value of tact tinged with humour.

Current chairman Norman Hart, a former schoolteacher, is a master of consensus as he seeks priorities for the second decade of a movement galvanised by undiluted local pride and continued national abuse of the authentic Norfolk sound.

We chatted over a cup of tea the other morning, comparing views on what has been achieved and what waits to be done. A shortage of young members and a need to attract more genuine interest from schools and the University of East Anglia topped my agenda.

Right on cue, I received a missive from the UEA asking for helpful tips for students staging Arnold Wesker's *Roots*, the play that put Norfolk on an international stage. I warned against the curse of Mummerzet mumblings and referred them to Friends Of Norfolk Dialect's splendid website for more enlightenment: www.norfolkdialect.com.

May opened with an evening of mardling and music at St Swithin's Parish Church in Frettenham with old friend Ian Prettyman. I included a Bible reading made in Norfolk.

Little wonder, really, that I count shuckety Shannocks, shoofs of corn and shuds down the yard instead of tired old sheep when it's time to get some Norfolk sleep.

DICKENS LEAGUE

January, 2012

It was definitely an evening of two halves. I left the Carling Cup semi-final first-leg clash between Manchester City and Liverpool at the interval, switching over to catch the second and concluding part of Charles Dickens' thriller, *The Mystery of Edwin Drood*.

This Victorian fixture went into extra time. Dickens died before blowing the final whistle on who exactly did what to whom in and around the musty vaults of Cloisterham Cathedral –although opium-crazed choirmaster John Jasper and his obsession for 17-year-old innocent Rosa Bud provided useful leads.

There have been several brave attempts to complete the job Dickens started. Gwyneth Hughes took on the substitute role for this latest television replay and mopped up neatly at the back while feeding midfield instincts for creative passing.

There are no easy games in the Dickens League. All his players give 110 per cent, run their gaiters off, make an impact early doors, show they're far too good to go down (even dubious signings like Jasper) and accept that while you can't win the title by Christmas, you can certainly lose it.

Perhaps you might see where this chance collision between literature and sport is leading ... yes, selection of an outstanding soccer line-up from the master's more colourful characters.

With home games staged at Dingley Dell, kit supplied by The Old Curiosity Shop, weekly match reports in The Hard Times, catering by Havisham Patisserie and match - day balls sponsored by Jaggers & Jingle, it's a combination tailored for great expectations.

Smooth-talking manager Sam Weller and his youthful assistant Artful Dodger are looking for promotion with this team;   Fagin; Gradgrind, Cruncher, Tackleton, Slammer, Honeythunder, Magwitch, Murdstone, Swiveller, Pickwick, Barkis. Subs; Trotter, Snodgrass, Heep, Scrooge, Micawber.

Academy youngsters Twist, Copperfield and Steerforth are showing promise but Quilp, Sikes, Pecksniff and Marley are available for free transfers in the January window......

I often ponder the use of our wonderfully vibrant language as football managers, players, pundits and supporters are encouraged to show how far they can stoop in efforts to sum up their feelings, often well before they've even worked out what they are.

How can thousands of fans make up "a 12th man on the pitch"? That is cheating and a steal from cricket in any case. How can a thrilling encounter be "a great advert for the game" when all available space is taken up by those pitch-side rolling exhibitions?

What's this silly business about defence-minded visitors "parking the bus" at the back? What self-respecting groundsman, sharp-eyed referee, part-time traffic warden or diligent turnstile operator would sanction such behaviour?

We'll leave poorly parrots and lunar gymnastics where they belong in the dug-out of banality and salute a crop of comparative newcomers to soccer's zany circus of performing clichés.

It seems every stadium is subjected now to unbridled delights of "squeaky-bum time" while any club in the doldrums has to embrace the prime virtues of "bouncebackability."

For teams who do everything but put the ball in the back of the net – still, remarkably, the main aim of our beautiful game – there's a get-out clause in the mantra "just a bad day at the office."

What's that to do with being outnumbered in midfield, outwitted at the back and out of sorts up front? Do hard-working folk surrounded by computer screens and water coolers go home and complain about poor promotion prospects, inadequate training, time-wasting tactics, weak management, blatant favouritism, wrong decisions and sloppy thinking outside the box?

Why can't teams have "a bad day in the classroom", ignoring every obvious lesson in the book, "a sad session down the pub" when they fail to get into the next round, "a rotten time with the plumbers" as another home banker gurgles down the drain and "a less-than-enlightening interlude on the allotment" as they fail to dig deep enough to avoid relegation?

Other sports can spill over into real life, mainly at the behest of trendy politicians who want some sort of excuse for setting foot on a level playing field. Too many seem oblivious to the fact that building on precious green spaces to "kick-start the local economy" leaves hideous skid marks on any development circuit.

Even in Norfolk these days there's more "kick-starting" than "hand-cranking", a downward thrust of the pedal making the earth tremble as the tapes go up on another round for the Tribulation Trophy.

Cricket's big moment comes when a venerable relative or friend is called to The Great Pavilion in the Sky. We take consolation in coating our respects with gratitude for "a good innings at the crease of life" whatever kind of strokes or levels of gamesmanship might have been involved out there in the middle.

Hang on a second ... back to football and a newsflash from Dingley Dell where Weller's Wanderers have hit back in a manner that may suggest the quill is still mightier than the sward.

They have pulled level with second-half goals from Magwitch (struck with real conviction), Barkis (always a willing front runner) and surprise substitutes Micawber (he knew a chance would turn up) and Heep.

He, apparently, refused to accept any congratulations from excited colleagues.

DISAPPEARING SKY

February, 1989

We're running out of sky in Surrey Street in Norwich where I work at Radio Norfolk. A sign of the booming economic times. Cranes quiver in the February winds. Just enough room to park and ride up there before congestion reaches the clouds.

Norfolk Tower wouldn't pick up any plaudits from Prince Charles if he dropped in for the day. I doubt if he would approve of much that is going on in dear old Norwich at present.

Radio Norfolk is housed on the ground floor of what I have been known to call "The biggest broiler house this side of Colonel Sanders' back garden." There's not much of a view to go with it.

Never has been since we moved in nearly eight years ago. But there used to be a little bit of green mixed with a little bit of blue as we looked out of the window, mostly to wave back to inquisitive folk who wanted to see what local wireless voices looked like.

Now another new tomorrow is taking shape opposite, climbing a few more feet every day. In fact, the developers are getting their own back with an up-tempo version of one of our old Radio Norfolk slogans – "We're all around you."

When I moan about the shutters going up and the last trees coming down, the bulk of my colleagues dig deep into stocks of sympathy for those who think all forms of civilisation might have ended when the Canaries just failed to reach Wembley in 1959.

Sympathy can soon turn to anger as you dare to defend the rural image which Norwich evidently still reflects to some innocents outside the area. (That must mean beyond the obstacle course they call Aylsham Road).

Of course, it is all a matter of comparisons. The city has changed dramatically since I joined its working throng two decades ago.

Traffic problems now mount so quickly that any road improvements are simply tantamount to running full pelt to stand still. Even so, they tell me other places are far worse.

With so much more development ready to roll in city and suburbs and the infrastructure creaking so badly, the picture cannot improve in the absence of a revolutionary move like banning all traffic from the centre of Norwich. (Why is that such an unlikely starter?)

Congestion, fumes, noise, delays ... inevitable by-products of economic buoyancy. But I wonder how far commuters are prepared to go before they give up searching for a parking space or, in more sensitive moments, a little bit of greenery.

Mounting blood pressure before nine in the morning hardly suggests a diligent, whole-hearted approach to the challenges of the day. Surely a more contented worker – one not ravaged by worry over struggling towards the office where the last parking space went 20 minutes ago – must provide better value for money.

Last week's much-trumpeted report, *Norwich: A Time for Opportunity*, published by the University of East Anglia Economic Research Centre, takes note of those who find it hard to jump up and down with delight at the prospect of bold growth by the end of the century.

"Those of us who live in and around Norwich must hope that economic expansion in the area will improve our quality of life and not threaten all of those things which still allow Norwich to live up to its motto of being A Fine City,"

Must we just hope without expecting any useful safeguards? Is it fair to ask if our far-seeing friends at the research centre really understand the Norfolk preoccupation for being different? Would not too much development, along with "better communications," put paid to that "desirable environment" they pinpoint in the report? Hasn't the tourism bandwagon careered out of control in other places with historic attractions?

Once called "The city in an orchard", Norwich is in serious danger of becoming just another refuge for the speculative builders. They can make their money and run, leaving those who live and work in the city, as well as the thousands who use it for the essentials of life like football and shopping, to wonder how it was all allowed to happen.

I return to a Jonathan Mardle article, published in the *Eastern Daily Press* in 1950, to find some perspective and comfort.

He said then: "We of the present generation ought to do a great deal more to conserve the beauty of Norwich. For all our materialism, we have at last learned to respect it.

"But we live in an awkward age, in which we are trying for the first time to direct deliberately and municipally the growth of a city in which beauty, ugliness and mere solidarity have hitherto grown up side by side and haphazard, dependent on accidental coincidences, private taste and private means.

"We have become faithful restorers of buildings inherited from the past, but we are so respectful of them that we are sceptical of our own capacity to build anything as good.

"In point of fact, there is more good new building, as well as restoration, going on in Norwich at present than most of us appreciate; but on the whole, Norwich to come is more likely to respect the taste of Norwich of the 1920s and 1930s for its open spaces – its parks and gardens – than for its buildings."

He concluded: "Living, it must change and be renewed, and not all these changes have been for the better. But it is better to build courageously and hopefully, even if not always beautifully, than to suffer decay."

Characteristic tolerance from an outstanding essayist and citizen of Norwich. But did he see them taking away the sky over Surrey Street?

DOORSTEP DELIGHTS

July, 2010

I may not rival Marco Polo – or even Michael Palin – in the wanderlust stakes, but I do boast useful credentials when it comes to fully appreciating what's on offer close to home. Let's hear it for doorstep delights.

My idea of a good day out can embrace a casual stroll up and down Cromer Pier to count the waves below, a more taxing safari along the clifftop path toward our faithful lighthouse, preferably in half a gale, and a bookshop browse on the way home for a cup of tea and a few more chapters of enlightenment.

Then I rise next morning ready to go native beyond the parish boundaries, taste for adventure sharpened by calls to continue mardling missionary work in far-flung corners of the Norfolk empire. With an occasional sortie into Suffolk just to see what they are making of this rum ole 21st century.

When we transferred the Skipper family seat to Cromer in 1988 it seemed only proper to plug embarrassing gaps on our "local attractions" visiting list. Now regular returns to those handsome halls and enticing grounds at Blickling and Felbrigg underline the sheer joy of noticing treats on our own doorstep.

No need to leave them exclusively to tourists with a feeling for style and history. Residents making friends with the familiar are just as important to the long-term future of our precious heritage as any holiday bandwagon packed with birds of passage.

That leads me inevitably to the Norfolk Wildlife Trust and its welcoming visitors' centre overlooking magical Cley Marshes. Over 300 species of birds have been recorded here, from avocet to yellow wagtail. I dropped in as the lesser spotted vocal yokel to spy on the freshly blown-in window gazer, a fascinating exercise that need not ruffle too many feathers.

I fought off a slightly uncharitable urge to dub them an up-market version of the legendary Walcott Wall Watchers Club, an unofficial gathering of parked vehicles near the seafront of this small but fashionable North Norfolk watering hole, usually on a Sunday afternoon in winter.

A bearded man in shorts sipped tea, munched sandwiches, scanned sunlit marshes with powerful binoculars and ticked off another item on his checklist. A couple in matching tops consulted their newly-purchased book of birds and wondered out loud if that really was a ringed plover.

I saw a Coasthopper bus saunter by when I wanted it to do a little turn in the car park below. It was hard to tell the difference between a miniscule insect crawling on the window and a black-headed gull out there on the horizon.

If you can't tweet 'em, might as well join 'em. I asked a cheerful chap in Wildlife Trust sweater when I could expect to see a whimbrel. "About now... if you head for Shetland or Orkney," he answered helpfully.

This large wading bird with longish legs and a long bill that curves near the tip only breeds up there but it's a passage migrant to other areas in spring and autumn on its way from and to wintering areas in South Africa.

Perhaps I'll catch up with the whimbrel at Cley later in the year if it joins other second-homers along our glorious coast. My new-found birdie buddy urged me to listen out for the distinctive call of the "seven-note whistler".

He reported a flurry of excitement at the nature reserve a few days earlier when Chilean flamingos dropped in. Apparently, a bit like hearing someone order a pint of Bullards best bitter with a broad Norfolk accent in a Lerwick bistro.

Don't think I'll ever make a fully-fledged ornithologist. I just like birds being there, singing, swooping, squabbling, scavenging and showing off now and again for people with patience, binoculars and notebooks.

We left this hotbed of reeds and Springwatch disciples for the cool and quiet of neighbouring parish churches at Cley, Wiveton and Blakeney. A lone robin on the wall by the kissing gate trilled a special welcome to Wiveton.

I peered across the meadows and the river Glaven to Cley and reminded myself this was once a tidal estuary with a quayside and boatbuilders' yard. Old rivals across the water.

June, with its strange cocktail of biting winds, soaring temperatures and nondescript hours in between, brought other ecclesiastical pleasures some way from our Cromer doorstep.

Bells rang out a welcome to St Michael and St Felix in Rumburgh. A long path, two sets of gates and a moat lie between the road and the church. There's a farm next door. All Suffolk charm.

Diss parish church makes any journey worthwhile – even a trek along the charmless A140 – while hearing thunder and watching lightning from the sanctuary of cloisters at Norwich Cathedral could prove to be natural treat of the year.

FADING BLOOM

February, 1989

Another petal has been torn from Poppyland's fading bloom. I watched with sadness as our impressive neighbour on the corner started to shrink, brick by brick, floor by floor, until it looked like a left-over from The Blitz.

The irony will not have escaped you. In the midst of the biggest building boom this county has seen, a boom clearly designed to offend my most tender feelings, I am preoccupied with the pulling apart of an old Cromer family hotel at the bottom of the road.

Wind whistling through windows without glass, and a doorway minus wood or purpose suspended above the rubble like a difficult piece in a giant jigsaw.

A staircase leading nowhere, but with tidy piles of bricks and tiles at the bottom waiting to be recycled. A crackling bonfire to get rid of unwanted evidence from the past.

Some order and some respect in work started before Christmas as men got to the chimneys before Santa. But demolition just the same.

The Craigside Hotel looked healthy enough as customers came and went last summer. Now the 22 bedrooms have gone, along with the indoor heated swimming pool and the sun-bathing patio.

The hotel trade is not what it used to be, and a host of boarding houses, also built on the foundations of the stirring Poppyland legend, have been converted into flats.

Simple economics, seaside-lovers, and constant reminders that gusts of change are just as likely to blow round The Garden Of Sleep as along the Golden Mile.

As Craigside crumbles, plans are drawn for a block of flats on the same site. No doubt, every sinew will be stretched to find harmony with the predominately Edwardian buildings along the road. Even so, those who knew The Craigside, either as visitor or regular passer-by, will nurse a little sadness, a little grievance, for some time.

I like to think Cromer, along with certain other parts of North Norfolk, can still entertain sentiment ahead of blatantly commercial considerations. I know how exploitation of the one led too quickly to over-emphasis on the other, but there has to be some soul left.

Even those who felt most protective towards the area when it first became fashionable must have guessed what was likely to happen.

Poppyland turned into Bungalow Land. In more recent years have come the added pressures of Caravan Land.

The marked rise in self-catering holidays has ripped out many floors from the old watchtowers of Poppyland. In some cases, an imposing exterior is simply a brave face put on for visitors, especially film and television crews looking for period pieces.

End of the line for an old Cromer family hotel

I must not infer every venerable hotel houses nothing more enticing or enterprising than a wedding reception for Miss Havisham – but they can hardly nurture great expectations in a rapidly-changing business. One suspects more converting, dismantling and, in extreme cases, demolishing are on the way.

It is intriguing to wonder how much hostility there might have been towards that building boom in Cromer towards the end of last century.

In addition to The Grand Hotel, the final decade saw the opening of The Metropole (1894), The Cliftonville (1894) and The Royal Links (1895) besides the expansion and rebuilding of the long-established Hotel de Paris.

There was a lavish banquet at the opening of The Metropole. One speaker congratulated the directors of the company which had built the hotel on their enterprise "in these days of depression". Another won warm applause by proclaiming, "the whole of the workforce employed on the hotel's construction were Norfolk men and Englishmen."

An editorial in *The Argus*, published in Norwich in July, 1887, spoke out for those who feared the worst about development ... "Cromer is about to prosper, to expand, to stretch from shore to distant station to provide amusement for the many rather than the few, but it is ceasing to be the Cromer we knew and loved."

One of the main targets for criticism was "the builder, the enemy of all repose, who leaves his red brick track on the face of the meadows."

Only three years earlier, a gospel of expansion was being preached with little fear of contradiction. Annie Berlyn, author of *Vera In Poppyland*, and a keen disciple of Clement Scott, the man who "discovered" the area, saw fit to declare: "Cromer is a place of infinite possibility. It is vain to hope that here all things will be as they have been,

"The time is close at hand when its borders, already fast increasing, will be greatly widened, when it will be even with other seaside resorts not more popular perhaps, but more populous and more pushing.

"There are those who grumble that Cromer built up and extended will be Cromer spoiled. Others there are who delight as they come year after year to find it hurrying along towards the inevitable end. It must come now. Such charms could not for ever be kept secret; their fame is spreading rapidly, and Cromer must provide for those who seek them..."

Sounds more like an excerpt from The Collected Thoughts of Nicholas Ridley! Listen very carefully, and you could hear more echoes from 1884 as the local tourist moguls flex their tonsils for Easter, 1989.

Annie Berlyn looked to the buffer zone for some refuge and long-term comfort: "But without, in the villages near at hand, and yet untouched by the rush and bustle of life, there will always be peace, there will always be the same calm delights, and hither the Cromer visitors wander in the long summer afternoons."

Always dangerous to use the word "always", and I am none too sure the likes of Overstrand, Sidestrand and Mundesley will find much room for Annie's forecasts.

Perhaps I am carrying old-fashioned sentiment a shade too far in conducting a vigil outside the remains of The Craigside Hotel. I never stayed there. We were just on nodding terms.

I recall getting misty-eyed when the old blacksmith's shed next door to my grandmother's house at Beeston gave up and keeled over one Sunday night after Chapel. It had been groaning for years, asking to be put out of its misery. But that did not lessen the sorrow when it went in a crash of dust, or dim the respect for the role it played in village life long before I was born.

Just because an old barn is sagging or tottering, you don't want to kick away its final days. A building does not have to be handsome to be loved, but I suppose it often has to disappear before it can be properly appreciated.

I enjoyed a mardle with The Friends of Cromer Museum after their annual meeting the other night, and five of my stories were taken away as potential exhibits. Most members of this valuable body have seen far more changes than me, a comparative newcomer to the town, and they glow with respect for all the bits and pieces that make up the area's past and present.

Unfortunately, I was a bit late with a suggestion that The Craigside would make a useful addition to their museum facilities. Perhaps it will be possible to catch one or two others before they fall – or get pushed over in the name of progress.

FALLEN FRIENDS

October, 1987

We are still in mourning for the loss of countless old friends. Fallen soldiers strewn across the Norfolk battlefields. Bemused starlings offering a ten-squawk salute in branches wearing Autumn's bridal colours for a shroud.

Leaves picked up and scattered like so many good intentions left behind by summer's sloth. A puckish breeze after that mad dentist of a hurricane uprooted so many years of natural beauty in town and country.

In some cases, amputation has carried the day over annihilation, but the damage done to our trees is all too painful to see. Previous planting campaigns will have to be put in the shade if genuine inroads are to be made into the devastated landscape.

A few savage hours of shrieking nature to mock man's folly in trying to chop down the world to suit the puny size of his urbanised ambitions. "This is how you do it!" howled the wind, bending, twisting and flattening.

We are left to wonder how many ceremonies with spade and public spirit will be needed to make any impact, and to dig into the past to find evidence that we might have got off lightly this time.

October 16, 1987, joins the list of dates destined for weather's book of notoriety. October 16th, 1881, brought its problems. The Rev. Benjamin Armstrong, Vicar of East Dereham, jotted down in his diary: "England was visited with a violent hurricane, which did much damage both on land and at sea."

Henry Rider Haggard drew a far more dramatic picture at the end of the last century when he peered over his shoulder in *A Farmer's Year* to size up the tempest of March, 1895:

"Everywhere trees were going down. They just bowed and vanished. One instant they were standing, the next they were gone. "But if it was rough Bungay way, other parts of the area, East Norfolk in particular, took the full blast:

"There the trees fell literally by the ten thousand, and such a sight as the woods presented after the hurricane was done with I never before witnessed. In some instances they were perfectly flat – a tangled heap of boughs and timber, and, here and there, standing above the debris, a deep-rooted oak with the top twisted out of it, or a great Scotch fir snapped in two like a carrot."

We have all collected stories of destruction these past few days. This one demanded a place in Rider Haggard's diary nearly a century ago:

"A friend told me that he stood in the middle of a little park and watched the surrounding woods go down, just as though they were being pressed to the earth by the power of some mighty hand. First the outer trees would fall, then line by line those that stood within till little or nothing was left.

"And the most curious feature of this marvellous spectacle was that no noise could be heard. Although forests were crashing to the earth all about, no sound reached the ears of the walker except the sound of that howling tempest."

Rider Haggard's poignant entry for October 22, 1898, is for me the perfect commentary to go with our best intentions in the years to come: "The reader may remember my writing of an aged relative who in her youth assisted at the planting of the trees which grow about this house. Today their autumn leaves fell upon her bier as she went by to burial. She was the last of her generation, and her death breaks another link with the past, for with her is buried much local history."

NORFOLK LOGIC

I like the Norfolk logic behind this explanation for so much confusion over the use of the apostrophe these days; "Wuh, what else kin y'expect wi' orl them dot-commas evrawhere yew look!"

June, 2001

FAREWELL WOOLIES

January, 2009

I was never very good at farewells. "Muir-hearted young warmint" hinted one village stalwart with that peculiar Norfolk mixture of admiration and admonishment.

She was moving away from native soil to be near her son somewhere in the Midlands. My downcast eyes brimmed with tears, not so much in mourning at the loss of a useful source of pocket money on the Saturday morning errands round as in sullen acceptance that I was unlikely to see her again.

She embarrassed me further with a hug that whiffed of violets and mothballs and a wide smile that promised she wouldn't let on about a boy with tender emotions.

It was our last meeting although I spied her, all crocheted shawl, long buttoned dress and hair in a tight bun, every time I biked past to other cottages and other hard-earned pennies.

That touching little episode from well over 50 years ago returned to taunt me gently as I wandered through Cromer and stopped at the end of a high street era. A constant from my lifetime was about to go.

I couldn't bring myself to join the throng picking gleefully over the Woolworth carcass but stood quietly outside to pay respects on a grey, chilly day made for recession talk.

Warming myself on memories of special visits to add another animal to my burgeoning farmyard or to buy sweets to scoff on the bus trip home, I had to admit Woolies was one of few big stores where I could pick and mix as an adult without muttering or moaning.

Sixpence went a long way when I looked up at shelves and smiling assistants in charge of little lads' dreams on Saturday afternoons long ago. Now they were ripping out the fittings in a last-rites frenzy and I felt a tear trickle down my chilly cheek.

Perhaps I was lucky no-one bothered to stick a label on me exclaiming: "Going cheap – one sentimental old fool". But a two-minute vigil on the pavement teemed with enough fond reflections to prove this was a tribute worth paying.

Village character and national retail institution, they formed vital parts of a boyhood world where change came as an exception to the golden rule of keeping life as straightforward and as familiar as possible. Crocheted shawl and Woolies are now mothballed in history.

My festive season surrounded by an old-fashioned family aura left over from the 1950s also called for poignant farewells to a couple of lovely ladies encountered along the fun and information highway.

Pat Bond, so smart in dress, manner and meaningful mardles, gave local Women's Institutes a regular and entertaining voice during my years as host of Radio Norfolk's Dinnertime Show.

She came in often after a hairdressing appointment to play to perfection the role of "posh" correspondent on a programme steeped in homely dialect and rustic pursuits. Pat raised the tone, the WI flag with vigour ... and then joined in any squit session going.

Love of the stage marked her as a natural for our annual pantomime on air, which she often helped write and produce, and special dramatic interludes in front of large audiences at the Royal Norfolk Show. She wore her best hat and put up with excruciating titles like "Premium Bond" and "Pat Ontheback".

Our friendship survived, blossomed indeed into regular correspondence – her upright handwriting was a treat – and cheerful reunions on the WI circuit. Pat's recent death sparked a justifiable chorus of rich praise for an outstanding Norfolk personality.

Kathy Staff's exit to the heavenly dressing room signalled the end of one of history's most celebrated unravished relationships between an unlikely sex symbol and an unkempt drop-out.

That's how brighter critics saw my cameo role opposite this wonderful actress in Norwich Theatre Royal's 1982-83 pantomime, *Mother Goose*.

"Will Nora Batty, the Cyd Charisse of Holmfirth, drop her broom and run into the arms of the Beeston Compo?" teased my old *EDP* colleague, Colin Chinery. Well, I got closer to those legendary wrinkled stockings than most.

Kathy Staff, the very antithesis of a battleaxe in curlers she portrayed in television's durable delight *Last of the Summer Wine*, paid me the supreme compliment of saying I was less wooden than most of the characters she had encountered while playing Doris Luke in the TV soap Crossroads.

She prayed in her dressing room before every Norwich panto performance of a record-breaking run. Some other members of the cast hinted she needed divine support when confronted by one of Norfolk's leading reprobates.

GENUINE SORT

November, 1987

I suspect there is little to be gained in suggesting that Ken Brown's sacking from Carrow Road will go down as one of the less enlightened moves of 1987.

I'll suggest it all the same because it makes me feel slightly better after a week in which respect and sympathy have tried hard to take over from anger. And it might help me to avoid temptation when the call arrives to become a football club director.

It is one of the game's more outstanding follies to perpetuate a belief that 92 employees can all be successful at the same time. Perhaps that's the only way to attract victims to certain dug-outs, but you'd have thought the word had got round.

Be they misguided, masochistic, mischievous – or simply blessed with a little magic – football managers don't last long. Directors, be they misguided, masochistic, mischievous – or simply blessed with a little money – usually give them a vote of confidence before swinging the axe.

Like it or lump it, that is the system. While it prevails, heads will roll with alarming regularity amid protestations it was the only option left after much heart-searching. The anatomical jigsaw continues as the latest casualty contemplates putting his knee in another's groin while the media are fed delightful lines like: "I'd give an arm and a leg for this moment not to have come."

After nearly 20 years of close contact with Carrow Road fortunes, serving local press and local wireless, I decided at the end of last season to step down from the soapbox. News of Ken Brown's dismissal made me ask myself if I'd experienced any sort of premonition following the most successful campaign in Norwich City's chequered First Division history.

No. Even after Mel Machin's move to Manchester City robbed the Radio Norfolk cricket team of a key figure for the annual match at Beetley, I didn't anticipate too many troubles piling up for the manager he left behind.

I have been standing back, listening to all the possible reasons for his sudden demise. I have read the letters, the majority, it seems, soaked in sympathy. The board have badly underestimated Ken Brown's popularity among the rank-and-file supporters and even those who acknowledge the existence of football only at times such as this. They know a genuine sort when they see and hear one.

Ken Brown came with a smile and went in tears

Let me declare an interest here. I broke the news 14 years ago on the front page of the *Eastern Daily Press* that John Bond and Ken Brown were poised to take over at Carrow Road following the dramatic resignation and departure of Ron Saunders.

Despite all the turmoil, City had pulled off a shock League Cup win at Southampton and it was in the boardroom after that tie I first met the couple who'd been making quite an impact with Bournemouth.

Southampton boss Lawrie McMenemey was generous in defeat and pointed me toward the leather-coated figures conspiring up the corner like refugees from *Smiley's People*. John Bond provided enough "wish we were there" quotes to fill three notebooks. His partner nodded, smiled and let the big feller do the talking – a pattern destined to become a regular feature of Carrow Road life during the next seven years.

Ken Brown lived in the shadows most of that time but played an important role in helping to keep colleague and club on the right lines. If Bond was too often the wicked uncle lambasting his players in public, Brown was the agony aunt comforting them in private.

He talked the manager out of resigning more than once. He laughed at some of his more outrageous ideas and comments to put them in some kind of perspective. In short, he fed Bond's strengths, worked overtime to keep his weaknesses in check and showed how fun and fairness could wear the same shirt.

For me, Ken Brown's most telling performance came in March, 1977, on the way home from Newcastle. City had crashed to a 5 – 1 defeat. Within minutes of the end of this one-sided affair, the players were hustled on to the coach for a brutally open seminar that spared no feelings.

Bond spat out barbed questions and ridiculed half-hearted answers. Whiplash rhetoric for over two hours ... I can still see some of the targets cowering.

Ken Brown was to pick up the pieces littered all over that bus. Quietly but effectively, he moved in after the storm to cajole, console or crack a joke where he thought it might prove useful. I swear he persuaded at least four Canaries not to commit suicide but to put on a brave face for Sunday morning detention at Trowse.

Perhaps he was happier and more effective as a coach and assistant but he defied those "much too nice" labels long enough to tell the doubters he did have what it is supposed to take to be a manager.

He never relished the after-match press conference like Bond, who hurled juicy quotes at the Fleet Street hounds and bared his emotions at the drop of a point. Brown couldn't be teased into talking away a bad result or gloating over a good one.

After Saunders the hard man and Bond the flamboyant, Brown the straightforward might have come as a tame act to those who make a living out of headlines. Persuasion isn't so eye-catching as bullying. Angry shouts sell more papers than genial smiles.

Ken Brown simply couldn't put on an act to suit the media. Perhaps he was a bit naive to think his simple, open virtues could shield against boardroom machinations and public clamour as bad results mounted up.

However, he deserved something far better than a curt "Well done, good and faithful Canary servant ... you know your way out". Ken Brown came with a smile. He went in tears. Fourteen years of honest graft in between. Like picking up pieces on the way back from humiliation in Newcastle.

Come to think of it, Ken, you should have followed my example at the end of last season and called it a day at Carrow Road. Would have saved a lot of anguish.

Now, just be careful in case hardened hearts turn soft and you are offered a seat on the board. The idea was mooted not long ago when you were one of the First Division's leading lights.

With last week's events in mind, do you really think you have the qualities to be a director?

CHALK AND CHEEK

A lad at a Norfolk village school inquired; "Please, miss, would yew be angry an' tell me orff fer suffin' I dint dew?"

The teacher replied: "No, of course not."

"Thass good," said the boy. "Then yew wunt mind cors I hent dun my hoomwork."

July, 2000

GHOSTLY CROCODILE

November, 2010

I was in town to celebrate the prospect of extra appeal at one of Norfolk's most beautiful churches. A short diversion on the way left me lamenting blatant lack of care and respect for splendid old buildings soaked in history on the opposite side of the market place.

A suitably eerie blanket of fog swirled over Swaffham, no doubt trying to cover up painful windows for sensitive souls bent on peering into the past. I stood at the gate of my old grammar school, doffed an imaginary cap and waited for the bell to clang as a signal to start remembering.

A ghostly crocodile of chattering boys marched up from the railway station, art and woodwork master Harry Carter acting as outrider with bow tie and flowing locks encouraging reasonable levels of behaviour. Thoughts of double algebra to start the week prompted a few obvious slouches when he wasn't looking.

I caught the train at Fransham and marched in and out of those gates for seven years. Hamond's Grammar School, founded in 1736, survived my departure until 1977 when it merged with the town's secondary modern to form a co-educational comprehensive.

The group of early 19th century buildings, acquired by trustees to expand the grammar school to cater for up to 100 pupils in 1895, served most recently as a sixth form centre. Now they stand, empty, forlorn, waiting apprehensively like an errant first-former cowering outside the headmaster's study on a bitterly cold morning.

Of course I'm biased and easily lured along sentimental corridors whenever those elegant buildings call up so many of my yesterdays. Old boys' reunions have offered poignant wanderings for those who can stand treble nostalgia where double algebra and single-minded masters used to be.

For all that, it would be scandalous to watch such prime-site assets slide deeper into neglect and decline. I assume some efforts are being made to breathe fresh life into this historic part of Swaffham, either as offices or residential apartments. When I last checked, the buildings still belonged to the Hamond Educational Charity and were leased by Norfolk County Council as part of the sixth form centre.

During the early years of the 19th century those buildings housed the Swaffham branch of the Norwich and Swaffham Bank run by three Day brothers, Thomas, Henry and William. The bank issued its own pound notes illustrated with an engraving of the town's market cross but went under in 1826. The premises reverted to a private residence for the Day family until taken over by the school.

Bought at auction for £735 by John Aldiss in 1895, they were rented to the Hamond trustees and became the school's boarding house and headmaster's accommodation with the original Campingland seat of learning initially being retained solely as classrooms.

Four years later, Aldiss sold the property to the trustees for £1,185 –perhaps he should have worked behind the counter for those Day brothers – when the market place site had classrooms added and the Campingland school reverted to boarding for boys and assistant masters.

End of history lesson... and on to an invitation to stride confidently towards the future amid uplifting company on the other side of the market place. Time to complete a proud double beneath a host of carved wooden angels poised in flight for over 600 years.

I was a patron 25 years back when St Peter & St Paul Parish Church launched an appeal to raise funds for completion of vital repair work. Now a new £250,000 campaign has started in the name of window restoration and other projects – and I am delighted to be back in a team of patrons to support the appeal committee and inspirational president, Baroness Shephard of Northwold.

My links with this church stretch back to Swaffham schooldays when we paid regular visits with headmaster, Major IEN Besley, in search of spiritual sustenance at the beginning and end of terms crammed with delights like double ...well, you can probably guess subjects on my list pleading for divine intervention.

I'll be presenting an evening of homely reflections, readings and yarns in the church on Friday, March 25 next year as part of a programme of fundraising events. A few classroom capers, railway reminiscences and mathematical mysteries are bound to be included.

The Pedlar of Swaffham was ushered towards London Bridge to hear about his pot of gold. I only have to turn up in town to be reminded of other treasures... like Nicholas Hamond's bequest of £1,000 to build and endow a school for 20 boys to be built on the old Campingland behind the church.

He died in 1725 and is buried in the north transept of St Peter & St Paul. I will pay humble respects next March. By that time it is to be hoped that a fog of deep uncertainty will no longer be haunting his name or certain buildings over the way.

HALL HAT-TRICK

March, 2011

There's nothing better than a return ticket to the heart of Norfolk for daring me to weigh up yesterday, today and tomorrow at the same time. At once an exhilarating but daunting exercise as such a balancing act can call for a bit more than native cunning and fond memories.

An invitation to open Great Dunham's impressive new village hall completed a proud hat-trick on my home patch following similar events at Beeston and Mileham in recent years. Cutting ribbons and unveiling plaques should concentrate the mind on adventures to come. I cannot resist knowing nods towards old-style community capers and characters past.

Still, it's only fair to start this three-way reflection by hailing the launching crew at Great Dunham, a potent fusion of hardy local and willing incomer, for taking on so bold a task and completing it successfully.

One of my pleasant tasks at the opening was to honour the driving force behind operations since he arrived in this mid-Norfolk village in 1997. Keith Mitchell, a former teacher in London and Oxfordshire, and wife Elizabeth, who has relished roles as midwife, district nurse and health visitor, mucked in immediately on "retiring" to the county they visited regularly for summer breaks.

Keith has proved an inspiring project co-ordinator and grateful committee colleagues rewarded him with what I described as "probably the most gloriously predictable surprise in Dunham history", naming the hall's meeting room after him. As I handed over a shining nameplate on behalf of a multitude of local admirers, I suggested Mr Mitchell had already proved himself worthy of that most blessed of Norfolk accolades – "He ent a bad ole boy!"

Singing youngsters from the village primary school – on my visiting list a few terms back to celebrate a library extension – reminded us how current facilities ought to be tailored to meet tomorrow's needs. The school is without a hall of its own and excited pupils were first to use the new setting for indoor PE, dance and drama.

Headteacher Sally Bone is also starting a breakfast club and other activities. "It's making a huge difference. Before we had to travel to another school to do indoor PE," she said, saluting the new hall's place at the heart of a community without pub, shop or post office.

I couldn't help wondering how many of those children on stage will be able to stay in tune with Norfolk rural life as 21st century challenges unfold. Secure jobs and affordable homes hardly top today's lists of countryside attractions. There's an obvious danger of even more good-looking corners being colonised by cosy cliques of the well-heeled and retired.

Mid-Norfolk MP George Freeman, a guest on Great Dunham's big day and an engaging mardler over lavish refreshments, is alive to such threats as he settles into his new job, although I suspect he may be pinning too many village revival hopes on an expected relaxation of planning restrictions.

It's easy to talk up A Localism Agenda. Perhaps it springs from the same think tank that gave us The Big Society. I reckon our county, still partially protected from hideous excesses by geographical isolation and homespun common sense, would do better to concentrate on The Vibrant Small Community.

So to the easy part of a return to familiar pastures, recalling childhood escapades by bike, some of them necessitated by banishment from my own parish, and making stark comparisons between our village hall, a Nissen hut on the old aerodrome, and today's palatial premises.

This inevitable wander down a hemlock-trimmed memory lane almost reached a gallop when I chatted to John Dawson, another Beeston old boy. His parents, Harry and Alice, were our Sunday School mentors for many years, loving stalwarts of the old Methodist congregation.

Harry was a local preacher as well and I joined him on many Swaffham Circuit chapel missions to chip in with Bible readings. A constant twinkle and endless supply of homely Norfolk stories collected on his rounds made Harry a delightful companion.

John, now well into his 80s, was among several given good cause to chastise my errant behaviour on the agricultural scene. My final Beeston harvest before starting work on newspapers in 1962 brought the notorious incident of Red Barn Hill when limited tractor driving skills were cruelly exposed by an unrehearsed Stirling Moss impression.

"Thetford journalist hits strawstack!" trumpeted a beaming John Dawson, his instant headline haunting me all the way out of an ill-fated flirtation with the idea of becoming a true son of the stubble. I typed that headline on top of the very first story I composed as a cub reporter to remind me of headlands left behind.

Oh, clean forgot to pass this on at the village hall opening. Everyone in Norfolk ought to know the last place to be christened in the county...

Records do not show if it was Great or Little when The Great Name-Giver looked at his list and sighed after over 700 little ceremonies - "Right, thass Dunham!"

HANDY ADVICE

January, 2011

Voices from the past can usher me purposefully enough into the future. Not screeching, preaching and fawningly beseeching voices. Just gently whimsical intonations drifting across the homely headlands to help me bed down comfortably in a brand new year on the same old terrain.

"May all your troubles last as long as your resolutions" has to be the perfect opener as we step over the shiny threshold and believe traditional customs and characteristics, virtues, vices and values, sights and sounds, are all safe. The Norfolk Way of Life must survive any pressures.

Threshing tackle may not throb on every farm. Sinkers and swimmers may not feature on every young housewife's menu. Some homes will never savour refreshing delights of well water or fragrant charms of the hunnycart. Estates are springing up with no respect for ferrets. I met a chap the other day who didn't know harvest festivals in Norfolk are large bloomers designed to inspire a chorus of All Is Safely Gathered In.,

Even so, our fundamentals cannot be broken on the wheel of progress. The millpond and the microchip. The yokel and the yuppy. The barn and the bypass. The turnpike and the tourist. The sickle and the silo. They can exist together.

Best way to convince the doubters, or at least confuse them, when they worry that things might never get back to normal is to suggest you are worried that they already have. A double-edged comment specially minted with Norfolk's cussed corps in mind. Don't let 'em know which way you're coming from or going to.

I remember a man rather full of himself finding it all but impossible to accept anyone should question his views at a village gathering in the 1960s. He turned on one of his critics and exclaimed: "You have a problem – you have no talent for surrender!"

He said more than he knew. It was an ideal summary of the dilemma confronting newcomer and know-all (not invariably the same person) when trying to cope with the Norfolk diehard.

A supposed put-down becomes at once a kick in the shins and a pat on the back. A snappy one-liner turns into attack in one breath and admiration in the next. Then comes the grand riposte with a disarming smile ... "Speaking your mind must limit conversation a bit."

There used to be two opening gambits in dealing with the Norfolk agitator always moaning about the rape and silage of his domain by property barons and other insensitive creatures. A contemptuous sniff or a patronising tap on the head sufficed to send him shuffling into a dark corner to mouth Chaucerian oaths and to contemplate his diminishing role as saviour of the rural cause.

Buy him half a pint, put it down to planning gain on the progress ledger, agree it is a hard old world... but that's the way the dickey crumbles. It hurts you far more than it hurts him.

It takes more sophisticated ploys to deal with a native uprising these days. Traditional protesting methods are coated with subtlety. For instance, many who used to think you had to shout yourself hoarse and turn six shades of purple to make a point now appreciate the value of a nudge, a wink, a smile or a well-directed whisper.

That should not be construed as capitulation. On the contrary, this marked change in approach can befuddle the opposition to such a degree it leads to strange little interludes of relatively peaceful co-existence.

Norfolk stalwarts, still slightly suspicious of the kind of progress that changes things, are ready to agree you can make many a false step by standing still but if you keep your mouth shut, at least you'll never put your foot in it.

Other handy snippets of advice collected on my working and social rounds go with well-tested proverbs dished out by sons of the soil during my rural upbringing. "Don't eat yellow snow" and "Never put off until tomorrow what you can do next week" came from one farmyard corner. "Always tell the truth – unless you're a very good liar" and "A trouble shared is ...all around the village in half an hour" emerged from the other.

A town councillor who relished a good verbal punch-up when the press gallery was full often reminded me: "Forgive your enemies – but don't forget their names." One of his colleagues chipped in occasionally with: "Some folk aren't like other people because they're different."

When it comes to handing out opinions, too many people can be very generous with what costs them nothing. One of the richest men I ever met used to remind himself and everybody else that if you had everything you wouldn't know where to put it.

Priceless line from a village shopkeeper to lighten our first steps in 2011. He told gabbling customers full of good intentions; "Best way to keep a New Year's resolution is to yourself."

HORSE POWER

Endearing characters making light of dark weather. Plenty of patience and staying power. Charming little reunions round bales of straw with cheery calls and nods of recognition.

And I got the feeling some of the people were enjoying it as well!

I spent time recently at an event organised by the Eastern Counties Heavy Horse Association Beefy showers turned into prolonged downpours.

We squelched through stubble, making muddy tracks towards winter. We scanned brooding skies to see if Will's Mother could provide any consolation. We clung to the hot refreshments stall for comfort. Through it all shone the unflappable qualities of magnificent beasts, ploughing and parading, working and walking, turning and targeting straight ahead. Like noble predecessors who ruled the old farming empire, they simply got on with the job.

Furrowing prime agricultural land in the rain at Drayton, on the fringes of Norwich and within earshot of grumbling traffic, had to be some kind of statement about staying true to countryside values.

Suffolks, Shires and Percherons took the same old challenges in their stride. As we frail humans in mechanical boxes struggled to leave, that adage about horse-power being safer and more effective when the horses had it demanded fresh inspection alongside the glistening soil.

October, 1998

HARVEST HOME

September, 2011

We bought three large punnets of Victoria plums gleaming at the back of a farmhouse all but submerged in a lather of flowers and foliage. A collection box for the money rattled thanks from an era when such automatic trust was par for the country course.

While my wife contemplated another jam-making session I ignored sharp showers to renew annual vows with Norfolk's rich soil by treading softly along a stubbled headland. I can now sing "All is safely gathered in" with a degree of smugness afforded that dwindling congregation of folk who actually set foot in a harvest field.

Bank holiday traffic building on the coast road beyond hungry flocks of crows and pigeons provided a last resounding crash of the cymbals before sweeter, gentler music ushers us towards autumn. My favourite time of the year, all mists and mellow magic to top and tail days it must be a sin to rush.

As cricket umpires remind themselves how it suddenly gets late earlier and Olympic hopefuls scan the horizons for new chariots of fire, we can slip back into the confidence of Mother Nature. The old girl doesn't change, just the circumstances in which she has to operate.

Intensive farming and chemical sprays have altered so many ground rules. There are fewer spontaneous thanks for bounty or the benevolent way in which it is delivered. Happily, there are still some rare beauties to take to the larder as the sun goes down on a freshly-shorn field. The throbbing combine, all dusty mayhem, leaves some charm in the stubble for an ageing howdgee boy.

Bales of straw become haphazard Stonehenges gazing sternly upon giant wheels frolicking nowhere on adjoining acres. Find a hedgerow seat and flip through summer's pages to savour a little sustenance. Take stock for dark, cold days to come in the warmth and comfort of preparing.

My harvest reverie had to include a chance meeting some 30 years ago with a long-serving son of the stubble in a village pub. As he sipped the last of the summer mild and asked if I was a "blow-in" like most of the regulars, he claimed to have a degree in countryside culture.

I was meant to ask for proof but it came anyhow before another lift of the tankard: "The coronation of the year has no majesty left. Harvest has been stripped of its ceremonial robes."

After applauding such a poetic turn of phrase I suggested the corn-gathering season inspired more romantic twaddle per row than any other item on the farming calendar. Surely he could accept the combine as a triumphant invention?

"Triumphant? Did away with scythe and sickle, horse and binder, thresher and thatcher, elevators and jugs of beer, children waving sticks and chasing rabbits, real and imaginary, into that bit left in the middle... a load of old romantic twaddle, by the Great Corn Dolly Parton!"

He was warming up nicely. I pointed out that even in 1900 on some advanced farms they had three reaper binders. Reduction of manpower was being brought about by the most basic innovation. Only a matter of time before numbers were cut dramatically.

"Yes, we saw it coming – the centuries-old tradition of harvesting, of gathering up the year's work, being taken away from the labourers. And we knew the agricultural profession would suffer on the human side. Trouble is, too many humans couldn't care less about that side.

"John Stewart Collis, poet among modern ecologists, warned us that gradually each man will come to work more and more on his own, neither able nor willing to take part in this, that and the other tasks in company."

By the Great Corn Dolly Parton! The harvest horkey couldn't be far away, boisterous jollifications bringing men and masters together in a common salute to the oldest festival. Did my learned friend subscribe to the school of thought that "horkey" was a corruption of "haut cri" from the loud shouting with which the horkey load was wheeled in?

"No, I think it comes from the hock-cart or hock-load of which Herrick sang:

> The harvest swain and wenches bound
> For joy to see the hock-cart crown'd"

He stroked poetry attached to the horkey bough. As they were carting the last load, someone would cut a green bough from the hedge and stick it on top of the sheaves. Then it was hoisted on to the stack, the last stack to arise, so everyone knew harvest was finished. Another link in the precious chain of tradition that connects a faithless present with the pagan past."

The pub landlord smiled kindly as I approached the bar for two refills. "Goes on a bit, but there might be a grain or two of truth in what the old boy says. After all, just how many kids today call them what we used to call them – the Harvest Holidays?"

I remember that old rural sage at the start of every September. His feasts and frolics don't go with combines and tractors and giant wheels of straw. Today's bare fields look lonely without the rick. There's too much room to sit and yield to yesterday's communal drive towards the coronation of the year with sickle and scythe as orb and sceptre and binder twine as bunting.

Wheels of straw at Booton

HEART OF NORFOLK

April, 1988

My affection for Dereham and its environs remains largely intact, despite some fearsome-looking arrows of development aimed at the heart of Norfolk.

Satellite villages like Gressenhall, Beetley, Shipdham and Scarning are beginning to wear that suburban dormitory pallor. No doubt, others will follow the trend before long.

The town itself, perhaps forced into a more self-analytical mood by the building of the bypass, has the inevitable problem of showing respect for the past while welcoming the future.

Dereham is used to the dilemma. I recall council meetings, public inquiries and agitated debates down the local 25 years ago when I was a young newspaper reporter in the town.

The overspill agreement with Birmingham and the urban limit map were two of the key issues as Dereham was urged to be bold and square up to continued growth in the next 20 years.

I remember the stark warning that the town would become an industrial backwater if development at South Green was blocked. It was the obvious place, said the new missionaries, a natural continuation of the industrial premises to the north – Jentique and Cranes – and the comparatively new Moorgate housing estate to the north east.

Even then, when it was not so fashionable to protest, some found it hard to watch trees coming down by the dozen to make way for the new post office site in Quebec Street.

Majestic sycamores and elegant poplars disappeared from the skyline and I had the temerity to ask workmen how they felt. A sort of intrusion into private grief.

"So few lovely trees are left that we shall be an industrial area before we know where we are," said one, peering down on a large fir he had just helped to topple.

Two weeks before that demolition, Dr A.J. O'Connor, retiring chairman of Dereham UDC, said at a council meeting that trees in the town should be better preserved and care taken that the town should not lose too many of the few.

A lot of yesterdays came out of hiding as I made my way to RAF Swanton Morley up the road, equipped with a good appetite and bad Norfolk jokes for a dining-in night at the Sergeants' Mess.

The base was on my reporting rounds 25 years ago as large crowds flocked to "Norfolk's answer to Farnborough", a two-day event believed to have been the largest civil air display held in East Anglia.

Dick Joice, of Anglia Television, opened the spectacular and acted as compere for both days. Pauline Cain, a blonde fashion model from Easton, near Norwich, was crowned Air Queen.

I made regular calls at RAF Swanton Morley in the early 1960s to see their Theatre Club in action. They won the maintenance Command Drama Trophy, with comedy their stock in trade.

On my final visit I must have been suffering from delusions that Kenneth Tynan's job was waiting in the wings...

"I am not suggesting that this well-established and highly competent group of entertainers should leave the hip-bath world of near-farce for the kitchen sink bandwagon, but surely the time is now ripe for them to try something a little more ambitious."

Yes, I was one of the more outspoken drama critics to be dispatched by the *Dereham and Fakenham Times*. The fact I travelled by bike simply added to an air of intrigue.

The Dereham pub stage also claimed my attention, but it was all in the course of duty. Thursday night meant darts, and I was cajoled into providing a match-of-the-week report for Sid Steward's round–up in Saturday's *Eastern Evening News*.

Sid, who celebrated his 80th birthday recently, could never rouse the same sporting passion within me when it came to bowls, still the great love of his life, although he would have been proud of that headline I conjured out of the story about the old George Hotel bowls green giving way to a new set-up ... "Bye George – it's St Nicholas!"

Thursday night darts dramas and Friday morning duties on the Press bench at the magistrates' court did not always prove the most pleasing cocktail for a young man at an impressionable stage of his journalistic career.

I did ask for Dereham League matches to be switched, but the committee persuaded me to eat more rolls and drink less beer. Most of the pubs provided a table and chair to make my note taking easier, and I treated landlords to dish out stern reminders that I had better by off to stand a reasonable chance of being up in time next morning.

I replayed several of those memorable evenings within minutes of arriving at RAF Swanton Morley and bumping into "Harbo" Studd who works at the base.

My bullseye was remembering he played for the Fleece. I chalked up a few more precious points with a roll-call of his colleagues – landlord Joe Head, veteran Reg Dack, window-cleaner Billy Hurrell, brothers George and "Brush" Holliday, Ted Cocker, Ted Wacey ...

The call came to leave the pub past and enter the Sergeants' Mess to sing for my supper. When I meet "Harbo" again we'll share a half and recall epic struggles against the Fox and Hounds, the Cock, the Bull, the Standard, J.J. Wrights and other sides with their share of outstanding characters.

Now perhaps you can understand why my affection for Dereham and its environs remains largely intact. The slings and arrows of outrageous nostalgia do help.

WELL GOOD

I forced myself to watch television long enough, like, the other evening, like, to find out what's happening, sort of, like, to our precious language.

Basically, I was gutted. Know what I mean, you guys? They were all walking the walk (presumably in pursuit of a level playing field), talking the talk and living the dream. Unbelievable stuff.

Actually, a worst-case scenario got worse, like, at that moment in time when a politician came on board. He was well good at saying "What we are saying is ..." and then saying nothing. I won't be downloading his podcast, whatever that might mean.

A man in an awesome tie put the wind up us for an hour and then told us to sleep well and not have nightmares. Fantastic. A woman with incredible body language said it was time for the news where we were. Brilliant.

Everybody else urged us to press red buttons, interact with total strangers and text madly deep into the night. Absolutely scary, that's for sure.

I was shattered, y'know, and decided to change tack big-time. I went to bed and read a good book. Take my word for it.

Redemption.

July, 2007

71

HISTORY LESSON

March, 2012

One of the most gloriously succinct summaries in history – or any other subject on my grammar school timetable – arrived on a crisp March morning just as attentions were wandering towards knocking off for dinner.

Cedric Dunnock-Staithe (not his real name), the boy with the broadest Norfolk accent in our form, was selected to bring us up to date with causes of the French Revolution. His lyrical response would have prompted hearty cackling at the foot of any guillotine.

He cleared his throat, always a prolonged and noisy performance, stroked his chin and offered every indication of delivering a lengthy and learned treatise on the biggest event in Europe before Captain W E Johns, author of the Biggles books, became a sanitary inspector for Swaffham Rural District Council.

"They dint git on" announced our volunteered expert. It took some time for master and fellow pupils to grasp the rich significance of those four words delivered in proud rustic tones. Then the nearest I've seen or heard to a standing ovation in a classroom saw us through comfortably to beef patty and gravy time.

There, stripped of all gore, intrigue, upheaval and far-reaching ramifications, stood a perfect signpost to one of history's heavyweights. We realised immediately that countless other major events lined up in our textbooks could be put down to exactly the same cause – "They dint git on."

Cedric Dunnock-Staithe (not his real name) pointed us eagerly towards the English Civil War (if any war can be labelled as civil), a whole raft of revolutions, the Peterloo Massacre, two world conflicts destined to rock the 20th century, the 1932-33 cricket Bodyline Series in Australia and occasional disagreements between Norwich City and Ipswich Town football supporters.

This acute failure to see eye to eye, to co-exist in peace and harmony, to make allowances for differences in others, to reject excessive tribalism, runs like a teacher's red marker pen through all chapters of history.

Of course, some tutors remain slaves to the curriculum and examination boards by demanding meat to go on bones, but folk simply failing to get on with each other from parish pump to parliament, from family reunion to the United Nations, remains the most pertinent and persuasive answer to any questions raised about unreasonable behaviour.

The ever-reliable Alexis de Tocqueville (yes, his real name) summed up the start of the French Revolution like this: "Never was any event so inevitable and yet so utterly unforeseen." He got top marks as usual for his essay –although his peers didn't realise he could have been referring to the Norfolk Historical Mummers' latest production.

While aspirations for "Let Them Eat Dumplings" have risen scarcely above the mediocre since rehearsals started, a full-blooded pageant is due to be staged well before the 250th anniversary of those momentous events over the water. Egbert Crimplesham-Smythe (probably his real name), who does his Christmas shopping in Dieppe and has been on a twinning visit to Rouen, is charged with finding worthwhile Norfolk connections with the French Revolution.

His first contribution upset the purists. They claimed Sir Percy Blakeney, The Scarlet Pimpernel, was a colourful but extraneous character from the cloudy world of fiction. His proud surname soaked in samphire could not earn him a part. By the same token, brave Sydney Carton has been refused entry to the fray. The society say they have far, far better roles to have done in a production that must smack of authenticity.

Naturally, many central figures will come to sticky ends and the chance to take an early shower and head for the tavern has its own special appeal. There's been no shortage of offers to play the ill-fated Marie Antoinette and Louis XV1.

Lengthy auditions in all parts of the county suggest Norfolk accents will dominate when the Mummers break with tradition as the time arrives to hear pronouncements, pleas and excuses from other key characters changing the course of history. Stand by to salute Mardler Mirabeau, Trosher Talleyrand, Drawlatcher Danton, Buskins Beaumarchais, Lorfty Lafayette and Rum'un Robespierre.

While John McEnroe continues to turn down the cameo of the Tennis Court Oath, the actor favoured to play Mucky Marat says the prospect turns him hot and cold. Hardly surprising when you consider he's due to be murdered in his bath.

The executioner will not disguise his Norfolk roots as he provides a quick rendition a la Singing Postman – "Mynd yer hid, boy, mynd yer hid!" Something really sharp from Cantley Sugar Factory has been pledged while 20 tumbrels are being prepared for action at Gressenhall rural life museum.

With polite but firm refusals from Norwich, Wayland and Blundeston prisons to get closely involved, the Bastille Day segment will feature a full-scale charge across a village green yet to be nominated and across the yard to a boarded-up garden shed behind a celebrity chef's second home.

Heady times for one of the county's leading cultural bodies. It remains to be seen what the French make of a production that owes as much to the Norfolk urge to tricolate as to the need to unfurl the tricolour,

Cedric Dunnock-Staithe (I can't remember his real name) should be there to see how they get on.

KEEPING BALANCE

August, 2010

The age-old question is back in fashion – what to do with all those blessed pensioners exchanging memories, comparing ailments and organising frantic fresh rounds of "hunt the spectacles".

I'm beginning to take this personally despite jogging along in the prime of senility at 66. New figures (I prefer older ones with homely wrinkles) show Norfolk is set to outstrip the national average for people aged over 65 in the next 20 years.

Good old North Norfolk, where they believe old age may be here to stay, leads the way with 28.5 per cent of the population made up of over-65s, and that figure is set to jump to 37.9 per cent by 2031, against a UK average of just over 22 per cent.

Well, more of a stagger than a jump and any outstripping may be confined to elastic stockings... but these vital statistics should command close scrutiny until the official retirement age is raised to 86 or the Home Guard is restored to the clifftops of Cromer.

Care and support agencies are worried. I felt a bit like a tin of spam waiting for a Village at War Weekend at Gressenhall as one official lamented: "I think the elderly have been put on the back shelf for years."

Back in the golden 1980s, when I gave up smoking, got married and failed enough driving tests to appreciate the enduring bliss of a good walk, this teasing subject did emerge from the pantry on several occasions.

I recall a 1984 warning of Orwellian proportions that Norfolk was in dire danger of becoming "a haven for geriatrics". One county councillor, obviously a young tearaway, went so far as to call for barriers to go up to halt the influx of retired people.

A couple of slipper-warming years later, Swaffham vicar, the Rev Kenneth Reeves, said the vast majority of incoming retired folk would be far better off staying where they'd always lived. "They should adapt to retirement on familiar ground rather than take a leap into the 'idyllic' Norfolk countryside."

At that time, retirement-led migration from other parts of the country was increasing Norfolk's population by about 5,000 a year. Perhaps a Sunday sermon or two might have been built around this text from the book of Exodus: "I have been a stranger in a strange land."

Then veteran local politician Les Potter, still courting controversy whenever the stirring spirit moved him, said bluntly, "I don't want to live in a county becoming some kind of working-class Bournemouth" as he opposed plans for another sheltered old people's scheme in Breckland.

More "geriatric" jibes at Yarmouth over an extension plan at Hemsby in the name of senior citizens. Urgent calls for a more balanced population, especially along the coast, to ease pressures on social services and community cohesion.

The big question of 1988 cropped up when Broads Authority planners backed a scheme to convert part of a malting into flats "for the occupancy of elderly residents only." Challenged to define "elderly", the planners settled for ages ranging from 50 to 60. Tom Chipperfield told the gathering: "In Suffolk social services we think at 50 we should start going round the old people's homes to get acclimatised."

The fact I felt compelled to jot down these snippets in my diary, along with several others since along similar lines, proves an important debate has not been completely ignored.

Of course, I could easily pull rank and claim my proud native credentials entitle me to be just as much a Norfolk nuisance in my dotage as during all those eras of staying put to get there. Advancing years, however, can spawn unlikely traits ... like tolerance, benevolence and amiable contempt for figures and theories.

Somebody ripe in wisdom suggested old age takes away what we've inherited and gives us what we've earned. So Norfolk will be better positioned than many to cope with the traumas and travails of deep recession, not just through traditional virtues of cussedness and caution but also by dint of so many residents having been there before.

Make-do-and-mend missionaries, armed with darning needles, ration books and tallow candles, will set out from the frugal north to preach austerity in less enlightened areas.

Keep-fit enthusiasts in sheltered accommodation will open their doors to show younger neighbours age is all in the mind. The trick is to keep it from creeping down into your body.

Beleaguered local services will benefit from retraining programmes for the over-70s to find much-needed community police officers, teaching and playground assistants and traffic wardens. All will be empowered to administer an old-fashioned ding o' the lug where necessary to save money, time and bother.

Norfolk is ready to turn the rising tide of over-65s to exemplary advantage. Other parts where there's no known cure for the common birthday would do well to follow suit.

MABEL'S MEMORIES

Christmas Eve, 2011

Mabel was robbed of her husband by one war and lost her son in the next. Arthur died in the Flanders quagmire of 1917. Gregory perished on the beaches of Dunkirk in 1940.

She dusted their photographs gently, a weekly sideboard ritual, gazed for a few moments on unfailingly cheerful faces and then reorganised the crinkled newspaper on her fireside chair. Pale trimmings trembled above the hearth.

It was Christmas Eve, 1951, an occasion fashioned out of a clear need for continuing austerity in most Norfolk homes. Making a little go a long way came naturally to Mabel, born into rural poverty as her parents fought to squeeze a living out of a small parcel of stubborn land while Queen Victoria lorded it over half the world.

Married at the turn of the century to the boy she sat next to at village school, Mabel stayed close to deep countryside roots as Arthur worked on local farms until he answered the patriotic call to arms. He left a wife and young son behind to join the big march towards mud-caked carnage.

His widow taught herself dressmaking. His son became an accomplished craftsman, providing furniture for some of the most fashionable addresses in Norfolk. Then another war, albeit with a much clearer agenda, reintroduced Mabel to pain and loss.

With no other close relatives to console or concern her, she decided to settle for good in Harnser Cottage, small but comfortable as it sat back from the junction between Billhook Lane and Sibbits Square.

Rationing and snowy weather had been her main bugbears since the war ended. She prayed each night for the ceasefire to hold in Korea and for people all over the globe to pay heed to the waste of two long and hideous conflicts which had dominated her life so far. Nearer home, she prayed for poor King George after his major lung operation.

While the Festival of Britain that year made no difference to her part of the world, she realised it did present some sort of faith in a brighter future for all. Mabel hadn't taken much interest either in the London Olympics three years earlier but knew they didn't cost the earth and were organised well in a city savagely scarred by war.

The Games were highly unlikely to return to this country while she was alive. No doubt that old devil of inflation would push up the bill a quid or two if and when that starting pistol sounded again in the capital.

Winston Churchill was prime minister again at 77. She couldn't help feeling sorry for that nice little Clem Atlee who had started to build a better and fairer country. Then again, she'd felt a bit sad for Winston rejected so decisively in 1945 after his finest hour. People had such short memories.

Perhaps politicians would one day go back to that wartime coalition spirit, putting national need and unflinching principles ahead of party interests and short-term opportunism. Mabel knew it was time for proper dreams when she had thoughts like these.

She poked the fire a final time. There would be no visit from Santa Claus although she would look again in the morning at those five cards spaced generously to fill her mantelpiece. Reminders of how true friendship takes time in its stride but picks out Christmas to stop and cherish it.

Mabel wondered how long it might be before the telephone or some other means of communication took over from the copper-plate handwriting she mastered in Miss Bulmer's class with a promise it would serve her well all her days.

Then there was television ready to bring moving images into the home to inform and entertain at the push of a button. There was talk in the village of sets to be installed in a couple of the bigger houses but she was quite happy at present to believe the best pictures were on the wireless.

She remembered King George V making the first royal Christmas Day broadcast from Sandringham to the Empire in 1932. She heard again Mr Chamberlain declare this country was at war with Germany and Mr Churchill's rousing speeches to keep up morale. Voices you got to know and respect whether they brought good news or bad.

She would hear voices and see faces on falling asleep far quicker than hosts of excited youngsters on this most special of nights. She could take comfort from happy family Christmases as a child, a bride and a mother even if presents were few and rich food in short supply.

"Long as we hev each other, thass orl that reelly matter" Arthur used to say in his proud Norfolk tones. Her father doled out similar sentiments around a sparse festive board: "Least there's noffin here what hent bin paid for."

Mabel smiled at such basic philosophies born in the dark shadows of struggling farms and the dreaded workhouse. Now, after untold sacrifice in two world wars to end all wars, surely peace, goodwill and a little bit of prosperity must follow...

"Happy Christmas!" she whispered to herself, stroked the cat asleep in her chair and raided the sideboard for a tot of brandy.

MIRTH MASTERCLASS

April, 2009

Ken Dodd's marathon masterclass in mirth at the end of Cromer Pier filled one of the outstanding gaps on my lifetime achievements list.

I'd promised myself countless times to exercise chuckle muscles at a live performance in this area by one of the most tattifilarious characters in entertainment history.

I knew the risks involved. Tied to a theatre seat by non–stop humour until milk delivery hours. Trying to tuck away in the memory bank as many one-liners as possible before the next torrent. Feeling sorry for unwitting stooges worshipping near the front. Feeling a trifle guilty for lapping up all the corn and joining in bursts of romantic song.

Still, achieving certain ambitions must be worth the odd little sacrifice along the way. So it proved as a memorable Monday night slid effortlessly into a well-tickled Tuesday morning.

We were let out relatively early through good behaviour, for taking seriously his threat to add another 10 minutes to the show if we didn't laugh properly at the jokes.

The 81-year-old comedy legend came out for the second half with sandwich box and flask. "Haven't you got yours?" he chided pointedly as we tittered nervously and peeped at our watches.

I treated it as something akin to a grand family reunion at which a long-cherished but slightly dotty uncle insists on launching into his entire repertoire of party pieces before a final chorus of "We'll Meet Again". A well-trod path – but you laugh just as heartily as on the first occasion you heard it.

Like all durable comedians, Doddy embraces his audience, confides in them and takes them with him to milk the moment together, even after a series of unlikely diversions into strange territory.

It was wonderful watching him come home to a favourite punchline after several minutes of ducking and weaving round bizarre images – like granddad in a vat of mustard used in piccalilli production.

Plenty of amiable jibes at the host town's expense – "Cromer isn't twinned with anyone. But it does have a suicide pact with Grimsby" – and the occasional lapse into "Hev Yew Gotta Loight, Boy?" to underline appreciation of the local flag.

He should know what he's up to after 55 years in a business hardly renowned for being kind to simple souls whose main aim is to spread happiness. Perhaps reluctance to be parted from dedicated followers is a natural reaction after so long and successful a stand-up stint. Hence endurance tests galore.

During the 1960s, when I haunted Golden Mile dressing-rooms at Yarmouth for chats with some of my comedy idols, a live show still created and sustained a real rapport between artist and audience.

Several stars had come to terms with a new era. They had honed their trades in the music halls and were now earning big money in television studios. One of my heroes, Jimmy Wheeler, confided one night at the Windmill that real entertainment belonged on a stage with an audience out front.

As he pushed back the famous battered trilby and tuned his violin, he chuckled, "They might not tell you, but a lot of them round here do summer seasons to keep sane."

The veteran performer wouldn't elaborate – "Ay-ay, that's yer lot!" – but I picked up several other hints about the seaside and live shows being good for your sanity.

Frankie Howerd, Dick Emery, Arthur Askey, Mike and Bernie Winters, Morecambe and Wise, Peter Goodwright, Rolf Harris, Tommy Cooper, Des O'Connor, Jimmy Tarbuck, Jimmy Clitheroe... such a list of laughter-raisers and how often they'd raise a hand to make you listen as roars went up for someone else on the bill.

I regret that I never saw George Formby or Max Miller on stage; two of the spurs behind genuine relief at the chance to catch Ken Dodd on his chuckle-laden rounds.

He's relishing a glorious late summer with its trademark overtime sessions testing supporters to the full. A few wilted and faded away on the opening night of his Cromer mission.

I met a couple during the interval who had booked a taxi for 10.45. "Make that in the morning" I suggested as they mulled over a fresh negotiating time.

The Master of Tickleology at Knotty Ash University has gone a long way to revamping an old adage. It now informs that the show must go on, and on, and on.....

MOLE MODEL

June, 2010

Miffy wasn't the best mole role model for lads of such tender years. He cared little for political correctness and even less for the niceties of social cohesion. But he surfaced suddenly and rose rapidly as a firm home-made favourite.

When our sons were young and deserving enough of extra bedtime stories I amused them and indulged myself with off-the-cuff yarns about a group of characters betraying obvious weaknesses.

Enter Clarence Coypu (persecution complex), Reggie Rabbit (too intrusive by half), Freddy Ferret (slippery customer), Stanley Stoat (weasily distracted), Bertie Badger (set in his ways) and Cyril Squirrel (nuts about himself).

Their little foibles, however, soon dimmed into nothing a good community worker couldn't sort out alongside the glaring personality disorders afflicting Miffy Mole. Impatient, intolerant, cheeky, churlish and oblivious to rules designed for him as well as all the others... no wonder he became a sort of cuddly cult figure of the early 1990s.

He had an early version of the molebile phone, a swish apartment on top of Cromer Lighthouse – much to the chagrin of relatives and friends left to cope with tunnel vision in the likes of Lawn Avenue – and a gift for wild exaggeration. You know, making mountains...

For example, Miffy claimed to have a second home in the Moledives, a model girlfriend called Mole Flanders and a playwright cousin who took a bow and answered to the name of Moleyiere. In truth, his elder brother, Boris turned far more heads in climbing up the local government ladder as a burrow surveyor in Molebarton.

Naturally, Miffy's appeal to little boys at bedtime centred firmly on a proclivity for shaking a muddied paw at authority, speaking his molecontent mind and taking advantage of any situations where a little craftiness might go a long way.

My main excuses for such early-evening anthropomorphism sprang from a deep paternal instinct to offer little morality tracts in a light-hearted context and a desire to prevent a long-held affection for such creatures going underground or, at best, being confined to my country scrapbook of childhood memories.

Moles, even those with rapscallion tendencies, can play a part in the modern world. There's still scope for gentle reflection in the company of sensitive chums listing to wind in the willows although more animated diversions along the riverbank of life are hitting home.

Adrian Mole turned a timely searchlight on teenage angst. Spurious specimens had dear old George Smiley scowling and working overtime to track them down in The Circus. Bizarrely, Dame Celia Molestrangler, played with gripping charm by Betty Marsden, encouraged us to think again about the big questions of life in Round the Horne.

See, I can rise above a penchant for moleapropisms and use Miffy's excesses and failings as perfect examples of what brought us blinking and thinking into a new age of harsh austerity.

Compromise will be a constant companion for the best part of some time. That brings me neatly to one of Miffy's bedtime contemporaries, What-a-Mess, a fat, untidy Afghan puppy created by comedy legend Frank Muir.

This canine adventurer thought he'd take a leaf out of the hedgehog's book and sleep away the dreary months of winter. He asked his mother to bark at the postman for him and then tried to snooze under the corner of the garden shed.

The cat, ever thoughtful, called to wish him Happy Birthday, Happy Christmas and Happy New Year. "That's three parties you'll be missing. By the way, your family's having roast pork tomorrow and you always get a piece of crackling. I'll taste it for you..."

What-a-Mess returned to his basket that evening. He hadn't given up hibernation. He'd decided to become a part-time hibernator – with an extra hour in the basket every morning.

There we are, a handy role model as chill winds race across the landscapes of our beleaguered lives. No need to become basket cases just because the going's tough. Find joy in little bits of crackling to fall from the table of hope.

I took such uplifting texts into a favourite Norfolk village churchyard on a day trimmed with sunshine, birdsong and a gloriously scattered rainbow of deepening colours. Proper mole country with a mini-mountain range twisting among the gravestones.

A man out of the beginning of a Thomas Hardy novel veered from his customary path towards cleaning the church and without any prompting provided a potted history of that building and the immediate locality and stories behind various churchyard memorials.

"Trouble with moles?" I hinted. "Yes, but we have a woman member of our congregation who can talk them away." He relished this dash of mystery added to a timeless rural canvas.

She's got plenty more talking to do. Wonder if it would help to tell them bedtime stories...

MR AVUNCULAR

October, 1997

The trouble with writing about friends and colleagues is a tendency to gloss over failings while polishing up the good points.

Then, on rare occasions, there's a sure knowledge that however far down the complimentary road you venture, others will be keen to go a furlong or two further. That is the sort of character assessment David Woodward attracts. Those who know him well invariably feel the urge to add a fresh verse to a familiar song of praise. He laughs it all off, tosses the halo aside and points to virtues in someone or something else.

Indeed, he changes the subject when his recently-obtained degree from the Open University is mentioned, but reluctantly allows himself a little twinkle when it is suggested he graduated in avuncularity many years ago.

He has worn that "avuncular" tag as a leading member of the Press Gang concert party and as a top-class wireless performer for well over a decade, his taste in good books as wide as the Waveney Valley. Now he has written one of his own, a career move destined to take his talents to an even wider audience whether he likes it or not.

Larn Yarself Silly Suffolk underlines David's natural feel for language, place and people. As I had no trouble in emphasising in my foreword to the book, he is the ideal choice to make learning fun for native and newcomer alike.

A comprehensive dictionary of dialect words is accompanied by teasing tasks and results, along with verses and stories to test that newly-acquired ability to speak proper Suffolk. Illustrated by Mary Brown, one of many old school pals to keep in touch with the boy David, this is a chirpily challenging stable mate for my volume Larn Yarself Norfolk, published last year.

Born in Beccles, the midwife cycling across the Waveney to deliver him, David hopped over the border to work on a Gillingham farm when he left school. He has kept a foot in either county ever since.

"I do have deep affection for both," he smiles, and you know this is no smooth diplomat at work, just a master of enthusiasms easily absorbed and liberally shared.

A passion for dialects and local writers has been at the heart of our lengthy friendship, with the odd cricket debate and exchange of views on bullace crops filling casual moments. We have exchanged homes as well, my growing appetite for Suffolk delights nourished by late-summer holidays amid the trees and fields of Frostenden.

I can now tell the difference between a rook and a crow, but I still agree with Agnes Strickland (1796–1879) in this appraisal of our close neighbours: "Suffolk men are so opposed to anything allied to change that it will take more than a century to render the portraitures of the present generation obsolete."

Without putting any bonds or reputations under pressure, I merely add a few decades and claim it is all down to Norfolk's stirring influence.

David Woodward, gentleman, scholar, performer, author and specialist in post-graduate avuncularity, is far too bright and/or polite to disagree.

David Woodward – twinkling in the Waveney Valley

MURDOCH MEMORIES

July, 2011

There used to be a Murdoch in the scattered hamlet of Lower Dodman. He imbibed nightly at his local, The Dewdrop Inn, now clinging defiantly to its hard-earned reputation as Norfolk's least trendy pub.

"Tapper" Murdoch won his nickname through an annoying habit of tapping his tankard on the counter when he considered it time for someone to buy him a drink, preferably a short after putting away several pints of mild. Few regulars were seduced by such subtle tapping-up operations and so he tended to sup alone near the open fireplace before The Great Landlord in the Sky called him home in the cruel winter of 1963.

His name and reputation, remembered only by the mature elite of village society, came out to be refreshed with a drop of ribald inspection recently as customers spent at least 15 minutes putting the big bad world to rights. Tuesday evenings after cribbage and phat invariably feature a current affairs debate hosted by a very common select committee.

This comprises retired coypu catcher Ernie Hoskins, retired stack thatcher Horry Barnes and retired muck spreader Billy Askew. There are occasional guest appearances by semi-retired dishwasher Elsie Wedgewood and non-celebrity chef Percy Pingle. Both work in the pub's Sinkers & Swimmers Restaurant.

Long-suffering landlord Jason Bullard, who claims running a rural hostelry is fast becoming as precarious an occupation as selling incinerators in the King's Lynn area, encourages plenty of verbal crossfire on the premise that dry throats need constant lubrication. He also accepts how earnest conversations spilling over into good-natured acrimony can claim too much valuable drinking time.

As a respected local historian with proud links to the famous brewing name, he often settles arguments before closing time, some of them started deliberately by him and Ernie Hoskins to liven up dull evenings. Such a little plot unfolded during the Murdoch debate. Ernie felt sure it was "Stinker" Murdoch who tried to cadge drinks before wobbling home on his old bike.

A wink to the bar brought mine host to the dispatch box. He offered a pickled egg and pint of that week's guest real ale, Booze of the World, to the first person who could prove Ernie was right or wrong. Horry Barnes said Ernie wasn't right and he could call medical evidence to back that assertion. He didn't want the egg but an extra half would not go amiss when he pointed out the difference between "Tapper" and "Stinker".

An expectant hush fell on the gathering as Horry unveiled Richard "Stinker" Murdoch who shared top billing with Kenneth Horne in the popular wartime wireless comedy show, Much Binding in the Marsh, a fictitious RAF station. In fact, beamed Horry, dear old "Stinker" was stationed at RAF Swanton Morley as Intelligence Officer with 226 Squadron in 1941-42 and played a leading role on the base's entertainment scene.

As far as he knew, he had no connections at all with "Tapper" Murdoch during that stint in Norfolk, although the Lower Dodman reprobate might possibly have wormed his bike down the runway and into the mess one night to try his luck with a new and unsuspecting audience. "If they were related in any way, I'm sure the famous airman would have had the sense to keep it quiet under the Official Secrets Act," added Horry as three halves of guest real ale arrived at his table.

Elsie Wedgewood asked if she could claim porky scratchings with a vodka and lime chaser for remembering Australian cricketer Keith Miller stationed at Great Massingham. And her grandfather used to tell her about the R33 airship breaking away from her moorings at Pulham St Mary in 1925 because he was busy in the little shed at the bottom of his garden at the time and heard it go over. Jason Bullard said he had shown quite enough generosity for one night but would use her memories as the basis for an aeronautical quiz later in the year.

Percy Pingle, subject to occasional flights of cultural fancy, tried to get a workshop going under the darts board as he revealed a passion for the novels of Iris Murdoch. "Not a patch on Mervyn Peake, Georgette Heyer and David Lodge," snapped a young woman who hadn't much enjoyed his samphire soup experiment earlier in the evening. "Don't recall seeing you at the festival" muttered a crestfallen chef.

Billy Askew gave him a knowing grin and whispered; "All right, ole partner, your secret is safe with me. I know you spent three weeks looking for a place called Latitude on a map of Suffolk. Nearly as good as Horry over there ... he wasted four years trying to find Tunstead Trosh on a map of Norfolk!"

With the Murdoch debate settled, "Tapper" and "Stinker" returned to the memory bank, it was time to concentrate more on drinking than thinking, although Elsie Wedgewood's threat to take out a super-injunction against publishers of the village magazine brought a few murmurs of excitement.

"I may have had my moments on darts club outings – but The Duzzy Dodman has no right to print that list!" she announced with all the vigour of a street newspaper vendor.

MY "SAFE HOUSE"

November, 2011

I've been ambling along Cromer seafront wondering out loud why they didn't regenerate me while they were about it.

Much easier to get away with that sort of eccentric behaviour this time of year when most of the people you're likely to bump into are either doing the same or are fully at ease with those who do.

Pier and promenade provide a sort of "safe house" from boring matters like where the next supermarket will spring up on the outskirts of town, when someone resembling a traffic warden may reappear on the streets and why so many shoppers have to ring home to find out what colour wrapping paper they want.

I suppose Sunday school outings to Hunstanton and Great Yarmouth in the 1950s nurtured that spirit of escapism as we sniffed annual rations of ozone, rejuvenated toes in sea and sand, made friends with donkeys instead of rounding up cows and invested nearly a shilling in slot machines to win a Woodbine.

Free for a day from the shackles of rural convention, we could ignore big-family commandments such as "Don't spend all your pennies in one go" and "Thou shalt not show thyself up by turning green along the Golden Mile after a crafty fag by the boating lake."

Even then, I noticed how many sensible older folk just sat and watched the ebb and flow of holiday humanity searching for the next thrill, another excuse to be a bit more daring than usual, a rare chance to wear a silly hat and a plunder a menu of candy floss, toffee apples and doughnuts. With fish and chips for afters.

I never sampled the seaside in winter until the mid-1960s when press reporting rounds took me back to Yarmouth as icy winds growled, angry waves roared and figures outside the waxworks museum wanted to huddle together for a spot of warmth.

So began a long-term relationship, occasionally bordering on flirtation with melancholy, between my more thoughtful moods and Norfolk's edge at its rawest.

As an honorary Crab since 1988, I have moaned about summer excesses like any self-respecting free spirit capable of seeing tourists as "space invaders" and then wallowed in winter expanses of time and room to ponder and roam.

That can hardly warrant a "selfish" vote, especially from those determined to shove an all-year-round tourism bandwagon into the teeth of fiercest gales, be they economic or straight off the North Sea.

It takes a special kind of masochist to yell "Welcome to Poppyland!" and do the job for them as a solo act entertaining rigor mortis on the end of Cromer Pier in the bleakest of mid-winters. I await my due reward.

Most glowing tributes to Cromer's enduring charms come from the summer pens of literary callers. Compton Mackenzie, famous for his novel *Whisky Galore*, is a prime example of someone who never knew the other side of the town's character.

He only soaked up the sun and mixed with the best, recalling in his autobiography how as a four-year-old in 1887 he found himself seated on the beach next to a "tall and beautiful lady" with heavily plaited dark hair and a notebook on her knee. She turned out to be the Empress of Austria.

Young Compton loved the surrounding countryside, fields of poppies and ox-eyed daisies which "always seemed to be overflowing from behind into the little seaside town" and the smell of honeysuckle in the July dusk "mingling its sweetness with the salty air."

Whether she visited or not, novelist Elizabeth Gaskell also managed an outstanding public relations role in *North and South*, published in 1855. She sent her contemplative heroine Margaret Hale to Cromer for a rest-cure. It appears to have worked:

"She used to sit long hours upon the beach, gazing intently on the waves as they chafed with perpetual motion against the pebbly shore – or she looked out upon the more distant heave and sparkle against the sky, and heard, without being conscious of hearing, the eternal psalm, which went up continually. She was soothed without knowing how or why."

Now, wouldn't it have been far more intriguing to see how young Compton, the jotting Empress and pensive Margaret coped with a few of them lazy old winds from the Arctic turning parasols inside out and rendering blue the most fashionable of seafront colours?

I pass a beach hut called The Shud and realise this is modern Norfolk catering for modern tastes. Boards to protect against vandalism and weather are going up all along our coast. Gulls decry the end of their takeaway season.

A couple of beachcombers melt into crouching shadows while festive lights burn in hotel windows above. A woman with a dog tugging her along scampers past as if bent on beating a dusky deadline.

There are times when I am soothed by these surroundings without really knowing how or why. I may hear the eternal psalm without catching all the words. Gazing at waves could be the perfect antidote to shopping.

I am certain, however, that our seaside in winter is good for the soul ... even if it has to be wrapped in several extra layers.

My favourite cliff-top walk in Cromer

NORMAN ECHOES

May, 2009

Mauve lilac dripped morning scent and fat raindrops. A crocodile of chatty schoolchildren sniffed history on the hoof between priory and castle. A band of water-proofed ramblers sheltered in a shop doorway to plan fresh adventures. Pub menus chalked on blackboards lined up for inspection.

Strangers entering through the bailey gate like men-at-arms and knights of old might well have thought they had stumbled across a carefully prepared film set to highlight virtues of a Norfolk community mixing business and leisure.

Few places in the county exude such a sense of ease and wellbeing as Castle Acre when it comes to welcoming visitors. Sharp showers bring a glisten rather than a glare, as befits one of the first to be chosen in Norfolk when conservation areas were set up in 1971.

It is a magnet for tourists, some drawn by one of the finest examples of Norman town planning in the country, and parking is such street sorrow even before the rust is upon the lilac.

Even so, you can still hear local speaking unto local in full expectation of a cheery response. We arrived as wind and wet mocked a previous week of enticing sunshine. Castle Acre kept on mardling. Perhaps it's a "conversation area" as well.

Arthur Mee, paying a visit for his Norfolk volume in the King's England series, first published in 1940, waxed lyrically: "Antiquity and beauty go hand in hand in this old place the Romans, Saxons and Normans knew. It lies on the line of the Peddars Way in a countryside where the long habitation of man seems to have exhausted the fruitfulness of the earth, so that blackthorn and wild rose spring where once were woods and fields of waving corn."

He missed the lilac. So did I on an early May mission in the 1950s for a Swaffham Methodist circuit rally. I carried the banner for our Sunday school – but sadly bore witness to the way a young mind can so easily stray from heavenly paths.

It was the Saturday afternoon of the FA Cup Final, the sort of clash I dreaded when chapel fixtures for the year came out. As we marched along those streets that owed so much to inspired Norman planning, I lurched dramatically towards an open window, my banner wildly askew.

Castle Acre – the village sign

Castle Acre – welcome to the history trail

Yes, the excitable tones of Raymond Glendenning commentating on the Wembley showpiece came drifting down a garden path to tempt me into loss of concentration. I pretended my shoelace had come undone to steal a few more moments of wireless magic.

My favourite Castle Acre voice belonged to Charlie Wilson, a passionate and powerful Methodist lay preacher. His stentorian delivery seemed too big for our little chapel, especially when Old Testament prophets leapt from the pulpit, but he calmed down and smiled more with a special item for younger members of his congregation.

Other voices from other parishes close by rang out as we continued our brief tour of High Norfolk... avuncular Joe Bly of West Acre, languid Clarence Howlett of Weasenham, animated Ephraim Manning of Rougham. He put pews in peril with a thumping "Amen!"

A defiant chorus greeted my return to Cromer, the annual Norfolk dialect celebrations attracting a customary full house at the Parish Hall.

This was my first time in the audience after acting as adjudicator for 25 years, handing out comments and certificates, and allowing my successor to "bed down" in 2008.

Colin Burleigh, in his third and final year as chairman of Friends Of Norfolk Dialect, has taken on the adjudication role with relish. His love of the stage as comedian and musician brings a delightfully entertaining edge to the "serious" business of the night.

One sad note struck with monotonous regularity is a blatant shortage of youngsters either willing or able to take part. I've heard several reasons as to why a precious tradition is being left almost exclusively to older tongues.

Many children think it is cissy, even a cause for shame, to speak with a Norfolk accent. The last thing they want to do is risk even more ridicule by putting it on public display.

It's not encouraged enough in local schools despite valiant missionary work by Friends Of Norfolk Dialect in recent times and signs of a wider acceptance that no dialect should be allowed to curl up and die.

Let's raise our voices and insist yet again that "dewin' diffrunt" must be more than a neat little motto for Norfolk.

ON RED CARPET

June, 2011

I convinced myself that a drop of capital punishment would not only underline Norfolk's incomparable qualities but also throw a valuable research light on a classic dialect adventure played out on a Victorian stage.

On such flimsy foundations did I try to build a reasonable excuse for placing the fleshpots of London ahead of the crabpots of Cromer. My wife packed my case, took me to meet the train and waved me off with the sort of look usually reserved for wartime evacuees or old folk who really shouldn't be let out on their own.

My early-evening call from a Piccadilly phone box must have provided some hope I might stretch for once beyond sheer survival – I didn't reverse the charges – or even threaten a place in the record books as Norfolk's most venerable new swinger in town.

It didn't quite work out like that. Natural shyness, a sore left leg, limited financial resources, an aversion to flashing lights or winking women and overwhelming tiredness after such an epic journey found me safely tucked up in bed with a good book well before midnight.

My role model from 1872 smiled at the prospect of memorable experiences to unfold in packed hours to come. I devoured the pages of *Giles's Trip to London, A Norfolk Labourer's First Peep at the World*, most successful of a best-selling humorous series soaked in glorious dialect by James Spilling, an intellectual who recognised the value of a homely and jocular touch.

He nursed the *Eastern Daily Press* into authority and prosperity as its second editor. London newspapers singled out Giles's' capital escapades as "not only the best example of the Norfolk dialect ever given to the world but also an admirable and spirited piece of farcical humour."

London, with its garish temptations and sophisticated ways, squares up to Norfolk's bucolic charms and gentle country pace, a sharp contrast destined to dominate dialect writing ever since. Fertile furrows still worth ploughing in and around the frantic West End as I compile a book on the subject due for publication this coming autumn. Giles, of course, will have a starring role as an innocent abroad.

A Dutch receptionist at my hotel grinned knowingly when I suggested all rooms should have a dwile to wipe the floor. Three barmen, a chatty Czech, an enigmatic Hungarian and a fanatical Liverpool fan from the

Philippines, needed only five rehearsals for a passable chorus of Hev Yew Gotta Loight, Boy? A Cockney taxi driver convinced me he knew people in Weasenham and Fakenham.

I bought an expensive floppy hat to protect my peeling pate from more sunny punishment and fall-out from a major fire being tackled in a 10-storey building on the Strand. Acrid smoke filled the air as I clambered on top of an open bus taking regular diversions from its advertised sightseeing route. My smart new headgear took off in a sudden gust on Tower Bridge. A chap in shorts at the back betrayed an unnecessary amount of pleasure in watching it decorate the Thames.

An old press colleague from the 1970s, who took the Giles trip a century later and decided to stay, lined up an evening treat in a London pub selling..... Suffolk beer! The Jerusalem Tavern in Clerkenwell is the capital watering-hole of St Peter's Brewery at South Elmham, near Bungay, and was voted 2009 Town Pub of the Year by the *Good Pub Guide*. The current building dates from 1720.

I considered South Elmham close enough to my Norfolk roots to warrant a home-from-home soiree with a binge on top. Chum Andy and two of his former Fleet Street crusaders regaled me with the kind of throat-drying yarns designed to keep pubs profitable in hard times and remind simple souls from Norfolk that it could be safer and saner to stay put.

A funny thing happened on our way to the Jerusalem Tavern. With diversions remaining in force after that big fire, Andy's alternative-route skills were severely tested as we ducked and dived around a maze of gloomy back streets. "Give Pudding Lane a miss!" I chortled to keep spirits up and demonstrate a useful feel for local history.

Suddenly we were caught up in a jostling crowd outside a big building. Only way through had to be under those ropes and along that strip of red carpet. A few youngsters cheered and called for autographs but serious-looking men in uniforms wanted to know where we were heading. They asked firmly but politely to see our passes.

It transpired we had gatecrashed our way to the entrance of the Theatre Royal as excitement mounted for the opening night of *Shrek the Musical*. Like all good pressmen confronted by embarrassing situations, we made our excuses and left.

Still, dear old Giles would have turned green with envy at the thought of nearly ending up in the chorus line behind a West End ogre. And I don't mean occasional Norfolk resident Amanda Holden stepping out as sweet Princess Fiona. She's got talent, excellent reviews and a proper sense of direction.

OPEN MARKET

January, 2012

While a few local headlines can raise eyebrows, like Holt being revealed as north Norfolk's child poverty blackspot or Great Yarmouth's historic jetty with Nelson links being deliberately smashed to pieces, many simply remind us what we know already.

There must have been a shrill chorus of "So tell us something new!" when the chairman of Salthouse parish council warned how his picturesque native settlement could turn into a ghost village dominated by second homes and way out of the reach of youngsters bred and born there.

Scant consolation for Salthouse in having a clutch of much-admired companions sharing that same dilemma along a glorious coastal run to Hunstanton as well as a few miles inland where Chelsea Tractors rule colonised acres.

I can remember fervent calls for more protection of Norfolk's home-grown virtues long before "indigenous remnants" became a handy label to stick on cussed old devils determined to kick up a fuss over who lives where and why it matters.

Council houses, tied cottages and aerodrome huts dominated a predominately agricultural village scene when I first started taking notice of my surroundings in the early 1950s.

We were still waiting for electricity and mains sewage but we had a school, shop and post office, chapel, church, two pubs, football and cricket teams, Nissen hut serving as village hall, twice-weekly bus service to Dereham and a railway line nearby.

Perhaps it was the last golden age of self-sufficient small communities. Many of my generation turned their backs on the land as mechanisation put men as well as horses out to grass. Old houses got the colour supplement treatment while new homes, predominately "executive dwellings" arose in the name of infilling. Mobile commuters and the well-heeled retired snapped them up out of what was still then a relatively sensible Norfolk countryside property market.

A curt summary of recent rural history, maybe, but it ought to carry some value when offered by someone able to make comparisons spanning more than half a century. And that does take into account an inevitable tinge of guilt for being part of the transformation.

Villages at the heart of Norfolk's ever-widening tourist trail have been saddled with most pressures to test the remaining local spirit.

Holiday lets, second homes, well-meaning missionaries and too many meddlesome birds of passage leave precious little scope for the sort of individuality and independence that once ran through coastal haunts like Salthouse.

Since that latest lament about this pretty corner being priced out of bounds for most locally born youngsters I've heard Norfolk voices, old and new, suggest it is high time they realised they've no divine right to live in a particular place just because family roots go down a long way.

"It's an open market. People can move when and where they like. You can't shut the door on freedom of choice. The days of Drawbridge Norfolk are over ..." A growing number of short, sharp texts to remind sentimental peasants to "get a life" and accept the inevitable.

Well, while parish councils are afforded so few powers, a major handicap for those under siege from within and without, it will be impossible to stay true to any kind of "dew diffrunt" formula.

When was the last time one of our district councils, let alone the county council, talked meaningfully about the challenge of change aimed at the future of family foundations in smaller communities? I am not resorting to the romantic when I contend such a topic had regular airings as a matter of course in the 1960s as village representatives met under a rural district council banner soon to be hauled down and banished as wholly unfashionable.

Even then, when proclamations of protection nourished local roots rather than derided them, countryside stalwarts knew there was no divine right for them or their families to stay put. But they demanded and expected a fair chance to do so.

Now too many slim hopes of extending family links and remaining in cherished spots hinge on the dubious benevolence of "affordable housing", usually tacked on as a sweetener for permission to build far more than site or situation warrants.

An overwhelming majority of developers couldn't give a broken theodolite for community cohesion or parochial pride. A blatant money-making agenda has no truck with sympathetic additions to what's already there or a village's entitlement to freedom to grow at its own pace to meet its own needs.

I am sure Salthouse and others forced into the "fashionable" spotlight by changing times, a hungry holiday trade and estate agents weaned on hyperbole will continue to look the part as Norfolk hears the call to cash in on the coming summer's Olympics-sized bonus.

It remains to be seen how many South American twitchers will descend on Cley Marshes in the hope of catching a glimpse of the Lesser-Spotted Norfolk Nonpareil or how often Australian swimmers and divers will yell "Cor, blarst me, cobber, that ent harf cowld in here!" as they dip a toe in Blakeney Harbour.

And there's a gold medal for the best Burnham dressed up as a cobwebbed corner where old eccentrics suck straw, shake their heads and pitchforks and mutter strange oaths.

OUR OLYMPICS

September, 2010

It could be several laps before the Olympic Games return to this country after our 2012 treat based in London. Even so, I am firing the starting pistol now for a concerted campaign to bring the most celebrated sporting festival in the world to dear old Norfolk.

The Olympics, too often mired in shady politics, silly money and scandalous cheating, need an overhaul, a new set of values, a fresh series of events in which ordinary mortals like you and I can excel. Norfolk must be the place for a new era to start as we bid farewell to Anna Bolak, Kurt Stairod and countless others soaked in jingoistic juices.

Perhaps the only floor exercise you can manage is scrubbing the kitchen tiles and individual foil means preparing the chicken for Sunday dinner. Maybe a three-day event is a weekend binge that leaves you with a Monday hangover and the hundred metres is your idea of a good working title for a gasman's memoirs.

The Norfolk-based Olympiad will be right up your loke. Based largely on the recent example of England's golden band of footballers in the World Cup, taking part will be much more important than winning, putting on a decent show or finding any sort of reasonable excuses for letting the nation down.

Croquet came and went in the 1900 Games with no apparent hoop of more invitations. Well, if Hunstanton wins the right to stage part of the Norfolk extravaganza, it could be back with a vengeance, a local team in Sunny Hunny boaters ready to take on the might of Australia, New Zealand and South Africa.

Tug-of-war made its mark in 1908. The United States pullers then complained that Liverpool Police, who beat them to inspire "Kop that!" headlines all over the tabloids, were wearing illegal boots with spikes. "We were proceeding with normal constabulary footwear," retorted the Merseyside marvels, suggesting that any more moans from the vanquished could lead those spikes into more fleshy pastures.

Reedham, home of the legendary Vikings line-up of more recent times, is the obvious setting for a muscle-bulging revival with no gripes over a century later, although Pulham Market will be pressing claims. As in 1908, rumours about Irish competitors being disqualified for pushing are bound to flourish.

While old-fashioned spirit ought to remain on draught, a big breakthrough could arrive in the shape of recreational winners we have known and loved since childhood. At last, all those hours of playground effort bearing grown-up fruit.

Marbles, hopscotch, flicking cigarette cards, spinning the top, bowling the hoop, sliding in hobnail boots (on tarmac and ice), egg-and-spoon (without chewing gum), three-legged race (including Long John Silver impersonators), long-chain tag, cheese rolling, sword dancing – perfect material for our free-wheeling Norfolk Olympics.

Plenty as well for the fringe festival of demonstration events with rural delights like skinning a rabbit, plucking a pheasant, bowling for the pig, drenching the wench, hunting the thimble, passing the parcel, tossing the pancake and pinning the tail on a dickey with your eyes shut.

Morris dancing, wellie-hurling, darts, cribbage, phat and dwile-flonking may feature, although ferrets down the trousers for scratch contestants and the four-horse hunnycart race for fully paid-up members of the Boadicea Woadrunners Club could face opposition from purists and health and safety sticklers.

Same applies to synchronised slimming, underwater fencing, bypass bartering, roadworks dodging, knockin' and toppin', sensitive hedgecutting, all-day drinking and Greco-Roman wrestling at Caistor St Edmund.

No qualms about conkers. Top of the Norfolk tree with our leading exponents fit to take on the world. Anticipate now a final showdown between our very own Deadeye Donny Dodman and the Iranian champion, I O Toller Rumjobentit on a quiet dual carriageway near Dunton ...

"Years of dedicated training now put to the ultimate test. The retired farm worker with his trusty seventy-niner and the former carpetmaker and his controversial eighty-fiver. Despite extensive tests at the IOC headquarters in Ringland, still no clear evidence that the Iranian conker is soaked in vinegar and baked in an oven on Regulo five.

"Silver is guaranteed for Norfolk. Here he comes, our conkering hero as Nelson's County, proud hosts for these, The Friendly Games, holds its collective breath while the bucolic man of the meadows aims to reduce the status of his final opponent to that of also-Iran.

"He stoops to conker! Ah, an old chestnut, I know, but we're going to yell ourselves hoarse for Norfolk. Come on, Deadeye Donny, give'im a Swar'ston wynder! Blasrt, he's orl of a muckwash!"

Homely fun with no awkward strings attached. So much better than a non-stop diet of diving and dressage, hockey and handball and weightlifting and water polo. Five rings under your eyes. Even London may shatter your personal best in the sporting survival stakes.

Roll on the Norfolk Olympics – with dewin' diffrunt on top of the podium.

PASSING FANCIES

January, 2011

It can be only a matter of time before I'm hailed as a medicated follower of fashion. Everything comes round again if you stay still long enough. Even on a dynamic catwalk like Cromer. I can wait with my old tweed titfer set at a jaunty angle.

There's always a small rash of smart new scarves, gloves, mufflers and other Dr Zhivago props breaking out on the high street to prove Santa knows where his haute couture bread is buttered. A snowflake or two riding on a puckish breeze can prompt a parade of trendy pensioners in fur-lined sou'westers, centrally-heated ski pants and moderately-priced green galoshes.

Brazen holidaymakers, some of them almost old enough to know better, greet summer on the Costa-del-Poppyland with a stunning range of long shorts being wobbled to death, garish shirts fighting for breath and floppy headgear bearing all the charm of a wayward pancake dropped from a great height.

Old comedians may say it's the coarse material that gets the laughs – but when the rush to be noticed tramples all over reasonable taste and self-respect, well, sensitive remnants must reserve the right to give the world a dressing-down.

My growing dislike for sartorial inelegance, especially when seaside strollers deck out little pet dogs in tight-fitting waistcoats from some canine boutique, could have its roots in a make-do-and-mend era when basic tidiness and comfort had to take precedence over passing fancies.

Post-war fashion tastes in the country seemed to be pinned largely on settling for what didn't itch too much. It was no cause for shame when your clothes were as old as your teenage children in the early 1950s. Mind you, hand-me-downs could cause a little embarrassment if you were an only son with six older sisters.

We didn't have baseball caps to wear the wrong way round. We did have knitted balaclavas to keep out icy winds and accurate snowballs. We didn't have expensive trainers and tracksuits to impress the girls. We skated into their hearts with hobnailed boots and flapping jackets on the playground slide. Few lads wore long trousers at primary school. We did slip into dungarees for messy farmyard chores to stop chapped knees frightening the animals.

Buttons and braces for boys. Pigtails and pinnies for girls. Fur stoles and mothballs for dressed-up matriarchs. Shiny buskins, trilby and a proper suit to set off pocket watch and chain for aspiring gents of the mid-Norfolk world. Overalls and a cap with peak at the back for milking time.

I remember a woman in our village with a passion for hats. Sadly, none of them returned her affection as she bobbed past on her bicycle, arrived late as usual at chapel, interrupted any conversation going in the shop or poured tea at every local function with refreshments advertised.

Her husband stood out as one of few men in the district never seen sporting any kind of headgear. The fact he boasted an impressive shock of dark hair, even in latter years, could well have dictated that aspect of his appearance. The bald truth concerning several others was plain to see at harvest thanksgiving services.

Chapel anniversary hats provided a dash of glamour along the crowded pews – a sort of rustic Ascot Ladies' Day with hymns rather than horses – while headscarves of all hues gave local sirens a hint of mystery, not least when they crouched and pedalled into a stiff wind. Looking prayerful and predatory at the same time, most were simply protecting a mass of curlers paving the way to weekend jollifications.

That's one of the lingering whiffs of childhood I can't get out of my system.... a home perm operation in the kitchen clearly designed to put

100

me off my tea as mum and my sisters did strange things with bowls and towels. I never volunteered to find out why "Friday night is Amami night." I agreed with dad that the only perm worth worrying about was on Littlewoods Pools.

Perhaps our new age of austerity will curb a few blatant excesses before a fresh holiday season beckons. I don't expect Cromer to be awash with boaters, bonnets and blazers. Calls for the revival of the bathing machine may leave the door open to a rash of smoking shelters on the beach. The sight of parasols could scare off the sun while crinoline offers little protection against lazy winds at the end of the pier. But a shade more respect for our proud Victorian and Edwardian heritage will not go amiss.

With playing days well behind me, I can now find a more genteel role for those cricket flannels around the promenade. A friend who knows all about style says I could go even further and follow the example of a toff from Sheringham who, when spring came round, used to write to his tailor, send him a small sample of dandruff ... and tell him to match it exactly.

TOP SET

Thanks for all your suggestions in my bid to compile a Top 20 set of Songs for Swinging Dental Patients.

This week's new entries are You've Lost that Lovely Filling by the Rightchewous Brothers, Gnawing Me, Gnawing You by Abba, That Old Plaque Magic by Frank Sinatra and Bridge Over Troubled Waters by Simon and Garglefunkel.

Shameless, I admit, but denture just know how bad this could get?

February, 2007

PASTORAL PULSE

July, 1989

Paddling in yesterday's waters can produce some unlikely reflections.

I rolled up my trouser legs and waited for cool confirmation that the old days were better. Finished with a lot of silt between my toes.

In fact, it soon became clear just how little anything changes. Walter Gabriel's old granny was quite correct if she did say there was nothing new under the sun.

For example, the pastoral impulse in Victorian England is being echoed uncannily in some of the forces and feelings of the current Green movement.

Our great debate seems much more complicated and has been elevated to the highest political level. At least the Victorians were spared too many contributions from that department.

High priests in their back-to-the-land pulpit, John Ruskin, William Morris and Edward Carpenter, merely had to put up with being called sandal-clad eccentrics who spouted slogans like "The plough is a better backbone than the factory" and encouraged girls to dress as Alpine peasants.

Perhaps the lasting value of their "alternative" pursuits was to urge future generations to question a deep-seated belief in untrammelled progress. Even in the late 19th century, market forces, working through a process of evolution to balance supply and demand, brooked no intervention.

It would be foolish to draw too many analogies between that era and this one, but certain similarities are most striking. The late 19th century brought a dramatic flowering of societies for protecting and preserving pieces of old England from urban and industrial onslaughts. We owe much to these pioneers who really meant it when they talked of saving something for their children's children.

Agriculture collapsed in 1870, prompting a big decline in the rural population. Much land was taken out of cultivation – again, we make comparisons with the present farming scene and all its eyelid-fluttering with diversification – and large tracts were given over to game. While the pheasant was ousting the peasant, cities were overcrowded.

A sudden rush of nostalgia for rural life completely ignored the possibility it could be tough, dull and lonely. As the new century beckoned, so did the rustic dream with a steady procession of urban emigrants to the countryside. George Sturt called them "Resident Trippers", underlining the fact that big shifts in population can inspire comments not far removed from the uncharitable.

As far as Ruskin, Morris, Carpenter and their colourful disciples were concerned, they made little impact on the overall scene. We must pray the present campaign, which has to go far deeper than an anti-industrial impulse, bears more green fruit.

At least those with the power to make vital decisions today in the name of tomorrow do seem to have accepted, albeit slowly and reluctantly, that not all environmental-conscious folk are into vegetarianism, flowing robes and a selection of Eastern religions.

On a purely local track there may be a strange sort of comfort to be gleaned from discovering that complaints we have come to take for granted were being made over a century ago. More uncanny echoes.

Bygone Norfolk, a volume edited by William Andrews in 1897, included this swipe at so-called progress:

"Of late years many interesting birds and animals once plentiful in Norfolk have become either rare or extinct. This is owing, partly to the better drainage of the marshes, the introduction of better guns and, of late years, to the invasion of a host of cockney visitors.

"Steam launches, numberless yachts, popping revolvers and champagne corks leave no peace to the modest denizens of the reed beds. Fowling-guns destroyed the splendid bustard that once roamed on the western heaths. What a magnificent bird it must have been, and how short-sighted its destroyers!"

In his *History of Norfolk*, published in 1885, Walter Rye pushed his prolific pen into critical waters as he came up to date ...

"It is painful for one who has known and loved the Broads as long as I have, in common honesty, to say that their charms have been greatly exaggerated of late.

"To read some of the word-painting about them you would think that you had only to leave Yarmouth and sail up the North river to get at once into a paradise of ferns, flowers and fish ... the first few miles will effectually disillusionize any stranger who has been taking in the 'Swiss Family Robinson' sort of rubbish.

"He will be disgusted with the very muddy flint walls up a tediously winding river dragging itself along through a flat uninteresting marsh country, varied only by drainage mills in various stages of dilapidation, and by telegraph poles."

Walter could never expect to be asked to provide copy for holiday brochures after that. So he kept on having a go. He noted on September 10, 1899: "I saw a beastly petrol launch for the first time on the Broads."

Intriguing to note how one of Norfolk's most patriotic sons was bemoaning the decline of the Broads over a hundred years ago, while so much other material painted a cosy picture of nature hugging itself closely. And you can still hear the same sort of contrasting cases being made today.

Four summers ago, *The Norfolk Landscape*, a volume glowing with sound perspective from David Dymond, reawakened us to the awesome environmental responsibilities placed on our generation.

As he sized up Broadland, one of the most important wetlands in Europe, he agreed the competing claims of agriculture, leisure and sport had to be heard.

"But at the same time, the fragile ecological fabric, which is infinitely more precious than any short-term economic gain, has to be maintained for posterity."

Nor did he shirk harsh truths in the closing lines of the book:

"Unfortunately, most of the successful conservationist schemes create no more than oases in a desert of mediocrity. We desperately need strategies and philosophies which will arrest the decline of ordinary, average places."

That's right. Before we are overwhelmed by global green issues, and the new, earnest pose of vote-seekers who know they must tackle them, let us take a quiet look round our own backyards.

Some were inclined to do just that long before the word ecology existed, and summit meant the top of a mountain. The poet Gerard Manley Hopkins, who died in June, 1889, spoke so eloquently for any generation or any era in which destruction takes precedence over creation:

O if we but knew what we do
When we delve or hew –
Hack and rack the growing green!

He was watching poplar trees being felled. He could have been looking at the ozone layer.

PERFECT EXCUSE

August, 2008

They still say about Wickhampton what they used to say about Norfolk as a whole: "You need a good excuse to go there."

Yes, those old "road to nowhere" lines get another airing as a cluster of houses on the edge of marshes ask to be taken seriously. This cosy corner deserves more than a predictable swish of the arm and vague "over there "in the general direction of Yarmouth.

We showed due respect in advance and asked the way from Freethorpe, beginning to look like so many other villages with a thirst for development. Wickhampton suddenly emerged down the lane as a model of rural restraint, small and neat, almost coy under the stare of a large parish church on rising ground. St Andrew's towers over Wickhampton Marshes, stretching out towards Breydon Water and Yarmouth.

I was breaking fresh soil with my ecclesiastical friends for another production of All Preachers Great and Small, our affectionate nod towards those who have graced local church and chapel pulpits over the centuries.

Cromer Town Crier Jason Bell chimed in as Parson James Woodforde of Weston Longville while former village headmaster Brian Patrick turned in another class performance as the Rev Benjamin Armstrong, Dereham vicar of Victorian times. They read extracts from their famous Norfolk diaries. Ian Prettyman provided musical diversions with melodeon, guitar and splendid singing voice. I read a Bible story in Norfolk dialect and shared favourite yarns. The good folk of Wickhampton and beyond extended a cordial welcome.

The local incumbent emphasised how this village used to be much bigger. "Now there's only one other public building, our red telephone box. We wouldn't all fit in there.... so we have gathered together in our lovely parish church." It stands as a memorial to busier times before drainage of the marshes in the 16th century. Grazing land for sheep farming turned Wickhampton into a quieter inland parish with a much smaller flock.

As the sun set over our latest outing, I reflected on the way "church" and "entertainment" have settled in the same pew in many priceless buildings on my recent rounds.

Ditchingham, Wortham and Gressenhall echoed to laughter and applause earlier this year. Denton on September 13 and New Buckenham on October 4 as part of that church's flower festival celebrations head the autumn list for All Preachers Great and Small.

I savoured a solo stint at Winterton with A Norfolk Journey. Thorpe Market's homely headquarters staged a "world premiere" when Boy John met the Singing Postman in February. Warbling friend Danny Platton shared the stage with me to salute two Norfolk dialect legends.

My wife took me to Sidestrand church, at the heart of Poppyland's unfading romance, for a telling mixture of local history and a lace making display. We went to Beccles parish church for a thanksgiving service to mark the life of dear Beryl Tooley, great-grand-daughter of Yarmouth naturalist Arthur Patterson. (Her sister Brenda played the organ for our Wickhampton get-together.)

Cool and refreshing, Cromer parish church has provided a perfect refuge on sultry Tuesday evenings for me since the beginning of July. The 123rd season of summer recitals continues until the end of September. My highlights so far include uplifting contributions from Australian trumpeter John Coulton and saxophone player Martin Thomas.

Martin teamed up with old favourite Bryan Ellum to present rarely-performed works for saxophone and organ. Their partnership reached a sensuous peak with Gabriel's Oboe (from the film The Mission) by Ennio Morricone, best known as the "spaghetti western" composer. Melody haunted me all the way home.

Back to Wickhampton for another lingering look at wall paintings in St Andrew's Church, rated among the best in this region. There are three of them calling for inspection as you enter through the porch, St Christopher, The Seven Acts of Mercy and Three Living and Three Dead.

Let me put a little flesh on that third one, an ancient legend depicting three kings. Hunting in the forest, they came across three corpses....... their own. The allegory alerts us to the transitory nature of this life with the skeletons' solemn message:

As you are now, so once were we.
As we are now, so shall you be.

Now that helps put in perspective major concerns of the hour like Gordon Brown's future, Max Mosley's past, Canary ambitions, Olympic dramas, Dad's Army celebrations, Countdown calamities, unitary authorities, affordable housing, public transport, binge drinking, women bishops and occasional deadlock in the middle of Cromer.

POETIC STOREY

October, 2008

What I know and feel about Fenland is largely down to Edward Storey, that region's most passionate ambassador for many years.

He provided a series of memorable radio interviews during the 1980s when I sought consolation among local writers over the changing face of our precious part of the world. Edward, mixing poetry and prose with infectious humour and common sense, created a vibrant refuge out of water and distance.

Spirit of the Fens remains for me the most compelling of his volumes, a personal and anecdotal exploration of local history with a foreword by highly-acclaimed Waterland author Graham Swift. He set his novel in the Fens "because they have a character and drama of their own, compellingly and hauntingly strange."

Swift deemed it remarkable that on the last lap of the 20th century there should still exist an area which most English people found peculiarly foreign when visiting it for the first time. Other admirers, initially reluctant but gradually captivated, have tried to get close to that unique spirit of place and unwavering loyalty of inhabitants. They can only agree that the Fens are not just a landscape but a state of mind, a mood, a human as well as a geographical condition.

Fenland's main chronicler of our era pointed to houses and farms clinging like crustaceans to the black hull of the earth: "Here you must walk with yourself, or share the spirits of forgotten ages."

Then, in the summer of 1999, Edward Storey flitted from his spiritual flatlands to the foot of ancient hills in Wales. He scoffed at rumours of retirement and accusations of forsaking those everlasting fields.

"I am a born-again poet, alive and kicking on the borders between two very different worlds, landscapes and cultures. I am gaining more by seeing the Fens from a distance, both in time and space. I will sing my song in a strange land" he told me in a letter from his new home in a hamlet scattered about lanes at the bottom of a hill in Powys.

Verses of that song came trilling through as Edward's genial company and uncluttered approach to the arts brought immediate involvement with his new local community, much of it centred on their delightful parish church in Discoed. Edward has composed and published three collections of poems in aid of St Michael's restoration fund. He and wife Angela work tirelessly for the cause.

Edward Storey, passionate ambassador for Fenland

A weekend of events to mark completion of restoration work is coming soon with old friend Ronald Blythe, doyen of East Anglian writers, joining the Storeys to help with celebrations.

Edward's most recent missive to me, complete with a batch of freshly-minted verses, relates a bit of excitement when chaps working in the church discovered a few hideaways. "They took up the floor of the nave, on which the Victorians had planted their varnished pews, and there was a complete skeleton. Not having a camera with me, I had to jot down a quick poem (copy enclosed).

"Imagine my despair when more were discovered the following day. A team of archaeologists had to be called in and they produced 72 skeletons, men, women and children, all about 350 years old. Well, I couldn't write poems for all that lot! The remains were reinterred in the chancel so they are nearer to the pulpit and can hear the preacher better. Victims of the plague, we believe."

Despite the absence of summer, Edward has enjoyed a good crop of poems this year with several featured in various publications. He's currently working on a play about Katherine of Aragon for a young actress with a theatrical group in Bristol.

As our correspondence ripens into a regular and eagerly-awaited exchange of news and views between Norfolk and Wales, I cherish a stream of verses demanding me to look beyond familiar hard-set boundaries.

Comparisons can often be melodious – both patches offer so much to savour – but there's growing discord in Discoed over proposals for a windfarm on an overlooking rise. Edward leaves no doubt where his sympathies rest in a poem called The Wind-Plunderers.... "We fear the tall ships coming over the hill, the marauders who would steal our souls as well as our country."

I will tell him about an 80-turbine development off Sheringham due to take shape next year. It has received vital consent from the Department of Business, Enterprise and Regulatory Reform.

Poetry in motion all at sea.

PURPLE SPONGE

August, 2011

I am going through a funny phase, finding it hard to take things seriously although, goodness knows, there's enough dark drama unfolding to force the most flippant Norfolk soul into solemn mode.

Perhaps it's the best way of coping with the rougher side of life, like listening to The Goon Show instead of swotting for tomorrow's exams, spending three hours in the pub before a showdown with the bank manager or reading Percy Thrower's autobiography when you should be digging the garden.

This latest bout of purposeful escapism began with an intriguing report of a purple sponge being discovered off East Runton, just along the coast from Cromer. I asked the wife straight why she'd been experimenting again with different hues of icing – and I didn't want half-baked excuses for adding to North Sea flavours.

Such culinary conundrums make me useful company at mealtimes once all sporting snippets have been hung out to dry. Joy knew few boundaries recently when I discovered "grotty coffee boy" is an anagram of "Geoffrey Boycott". Couldn't happen to a better-natured, modesty-blessed cricket authority. Even puts "Alec Guinness" equals "genuine class" in the shade.

Back to action from the Gastronomic End and a reasonable question from someone who feels too many cooks spill the broth, particularly over television menus – what exactly are "food heroes"?

I have been struggling to find any meaningful connection between substance taken into the body to maintain life and growth and someone admired for stirring deeds and noble qualities. Well, Gordon Ramsay isn't the first wholesome combination to pop out of the oven and Fanny Craddock could let herself down with second helpings of sarcasm dipped in scary looks.

I tried to imagine "food heroes" in the guise of masked crusaders fighting off killer kale, lethal leeks and spontaneously-combusting sprouts. I wandered back to an English lesson at grammar school in 1956 destined to put me off garden centres for life.

The Day of the Triffids introduced tall perambulating plants capable of aggressive and seemingly intelligent behaviour but bent on world domination. Teacher tried to laugh it off by suggesting they were no more dangerous than the Paston Lettuce (he was widely read) but the damage had been done.

Hogweed-picking missions to feed my pet rabbits suddenly grew fraught with menace. I steered clear of the family plot as battalions of runner beans started nocturnal manoeuvres. A cloche in the corner turned into a laboratory where mad scientists cloned an army of persecuting parsnips. I sensed the scarecrow down the lane was being cultivated as a spy who came alive after dark.

Out of desperation I sent for Dick Turnip, Norfolk's very own dyslexic highwayman, even though his credentials teetered on the side of unhelpful. Once he thought he'd reached Birmingham on Bleck Bass only to discover he'd spent the night at Briningham, near Holt.

Years passed and some Norfolk people were phonetically modified to help produce a better crop of "food heroes" despite a marked lack of information as to where the label came from and what it meant. Dick Turnip married a travelling midwife in Banningham (or Barningham) after inviting her to stand and deliver.

As usual, I found solace and enlightenment through homely culture rather than horticulture. A gentle stroll among my favourite books and films could help you do the same. A fair sprinkling of imagination will spice up the exercise and leave you hungry for afters.

My healthy diet had to begin with Goodbye Mr Chips, starring Robert Doughnut, the epicurean Lord of the Onion Rings and Moby Duck. Here come the Colander Girls rehearsing for Salad Days closely pursued by Three Men in a Gravy Boat and James Stewart pitching for Baker of the Year in It's a Wonderful Loaf.

Spaghetti westerns may not be good for you but gritty sons of the saddle like Butch Casserole, Davy Croquette and Tex Fritter deserve places at the "food heroes" table or even in a bunfight at the OK Corral.

Al Capon invites himself to any spread where "fowl play" is suspected while Raymond Chandler leads the hard-boiled fiction parade with an admission that his Farewell My Lovely might so easily have arrived in more saucy attire as Tartare My Bewty.

Good meaty reads on the classics shelf include Lady Chitterlings' Lover, Mansfield Pork, Hound of the Basketmeals and The Lunchpack of Notre Dame. Agatha Christie takes it a stage further with the long-running Moussetrap.

As you sniff adventure and think about compiling tasty little lists of your own – film stars (Sandra Bullock), sporting personalities (Allan Lamb) and politicians (Edwina Currie) for starters – I must call for one moment of reflection.

Those of a certain age can remember wartime rationing and years of shortages after that. Families made a lot out of a little with home-made delights like giant apple dumplings boiled in a cloth, bubble and squeak straight from the frying pan and all the bottled fruit you could eat.

"Waste not, want not" referred as much to time together as to household victuals. Did not that period of austerity more deserve awards for genuine family sustenance than the current era of celebrity chefs and bloated television offerings?

Oh dear, I'm turning all serious again.......

REUNION FUN

May, 2011

Old habits die hard. I left my history homework until a few hours before an annual reunion packed with little tests on dates and events. Thankfully, it is now more of a pleasure to be kept behind for extra swotting about the past. And we sampled a special cake to remind us of one special anniversary.

Over 120 "grammar grubs" and their guests rolled back the years at Swaffham's George Hotel, scene of an emotional get-together in the summer of 1986 to mark the 250th birthday of the town's Hamond's School. One of the key themes of that occasion was a determination to re-establish a group for those former pupils anxious to put sheen on the dullest of days and to prove that not everything went in one ear and out the other.

Ten of the old grammar school boys present had also attended the dinner at which the 200th anniversary was celebrated in 1936. High point of the bicentenary beano was a luncheon in the school hall, with tickets selling at half-a-crown (12½ pence), followed by a rugby match between the school XV and an old boys' side. In the evening, the ladies came in for dancing and whist.

While my maths record at Hamond's may suggest my days in such an enlightened establishment ought to have been numbered, I reckon we were marking two significant milestones at our latest gathering – the 275th birthday of the old school and the 25th anniversary of the Old Hamondians' Association. After initial struggles to rouse former troops into meaningful action, the eagerly-awaited annual reunion and regular newsletter underline why we can now have our cake and eat it.

Much of the credit for what headmaster Major IEN Besley would have described as "purposeful progress" goes to secretary Ted Heath, an unflappable character with neat lines in quiet diplomacy, gentle humour and deep respect for finer feelings. All these came together in his introduction to a recent newsletter when he thanked a former Latin and Music master for his generous donation to association funds.

"I will remember him for his teaching, his kindness and courtesy. I have already apologised to him directly for my own misbehaviour but since schooldays I have come to appreciate more fully the value of Latin towards improving one's English and giving one a better understanding of our language."

Ted uncovered a quote to encompass his failings while providing a glance at his endeavours: "English usage is sometimes more than mere taste, judgement and education – sometimes it's sheer luck, like getting across the street."

I savoured an unlikely discovery at last weekend's reunion when one of the brightest lads of my era in Swaffham - he collected top marks, distinctions and certificates like some of us lesser mortals collected stamps or reminders in red ink to see Sir later – admitted that I had scored a clear victory over him when it came to finding our first jobs on leaving school in 1962.

We both applied to the Norfolk News Company after an inspiring classroom visit from Eric Fowler, already a literary legend with his Jonathan Mardle essays in the *Eastern Daily Press*. I was taken on as a cub reporter pounding the mean streets of Thetford. My sixth-form colleague had to console himself with a career on national newspapers, including a distinguished spell with *The Times*.

I told him the local press might have gone more for likely potential and a homely Norfolk accent rather than sparkling achievement and well-modulated tones. In short, he peaked too early and talked too proper. And he probably had too many qualifications for weddings, funerals, whist drives, rural district council meetings, magistrates' courts – and annual reunions.

Just to show the magic is still there when it comes to extra history homework, I put myself in the mood for our good old days with a bit of digging and delving to find out what else was going on in 1736 as our seat of learning was being established.

Pope Clement X11 issued a bull condemning freemasonry. Britain repealed statutes against witchcraft after centuries of oppressing women, many of them midwives who competed with physicians. Physicist Gabriel Fahrenheit felt a few degrees under and died at The Hague aged 50.

A bathing establishment opened at Scarborough and other seaside communities soon followed. Horse-drawn machines took bathers out to a suitable depth where women in costumes scrambled out through a "modesty" hood into the arms of strong local women, known as "dippers", who taught their customers how to dogpaddle.

With all soccer promotion and relegation matters settled, cricket got a look-in with a big single-wicket match on Kennington Common, Mr Wakeland, the distiller, and Mr George Oldner taking on two "famous" Richmond players. Records do not name the esteemed pair although one of them suffered serious facial injuries when the ball flew off his bat and struck his nose.

The 1736 sports reporter railed against "human brutes" who insisted he should play on despite his injuries. Well, there was good money riding on the result, a little consideration often taking priority during the last 275 years.

SALTY ADVENTURER

May, 2010

He looked and sounded like a refugee from Treasure Island. Gingery beard, muscular frame, booming voice, piercing eyes darting from menace to mirth in no time and a throaty chortle to clear the decks for another salty adventure.

Richard Davies was halfway through his 23-year stint as Cromer lifeboat coxswain when we moved our family seat to the town in 1988. He greeted me with a nerve-numbing slap on the back and a clear warning not to stray too far into choppy waters.

We had met several times before on my own media foreshore, the radio studio, where he revelled in sailing as close as possible to puckish winds. A blissfully blunt response to all matter of questions marked him as an innovative and exciting if rather dangerous guest for a live interview.

Richard's unyielding rejection of political correctness could be camouflaged with cheery banter and sudden switches in direction, but he sensed you liked him and his material so much that all transgressions could be forgotten by the end of transmission.

While soppy landlubbers like me struggled to keep a rein on his wild rover personality, Cromer's man at the helm did yield occasionally to the calming charms of his Sheringham counterpart.

One of my abiding broadcasting memories settles on a bank holiday special reflecting mutual affection and respect between Daredevil Davies and Personable Pegg as they dealt smoothly with their Crab Wars legacy. Contrasting characters meeting comfortably and amusingly in the middle.

Brian Pegg, Salvation Army stalwart and one of a select few to be allowed free passage over the border without an armed escort, steered his old friend into unlikely waters with homely comparisons and subtle suggestions. A double act of whom north Norfolk as a whole could be proud.

Reliable reports suggest Richard Davies was "a bit of a rum'un" as a young man. Some may take that as Norfolk shorthand for "hellraiser" and he did admit to me one Sunday morning on the front that he much preferred a sou'wester on his head to a halo hovering above it.

He shunned "hero" talk despite awards for bravery during nearly 40 years of service to the RNLI. Just as significantly, he refused to play the "celebrity seafarer" game in an era when it became increasingly common for anyone of note within 20 miles of the Burnhams to chase the passing spotlight.

Richard didn't quite make the full transition from rumbustious young buck to venerable old salt – he died recently at 65 from a brain tumour – but I suggest he would have continued to write his own script and deliver it how and when he liked.

His nautical knowledge was fathoms deep, hardly surprising in light of a family dynasty whose connections with lifesaving at sea stretch back two centuries, and he loved to share it with "serious" television programmes like *Timewatch*. With great uncles like Henry Blogg and Henry "Shrimp" Davies, the boy Richard had to get used to feeling at home with proud traditions.

For a man with so much sea in his blood, Richard found a surprising amount of scope for country pursuits. I mustered enough courage one Sunday morning to question his support for hare coursing – a "sport" I abhor – but he refused to be drawn. He hurled a big arm round my comparatively puny shoulder and chuckled: "Each to his own, boy, each to his own."

We found happy common ground on stage as his extrovert nature and delicious lightness of foot kept traditional step dancing to the fore. He answered calls to give special displays at Mundesley Festival and on my Press Gang farewell entertainment rounds.

Richard Davies stepping out

Our final flourish together came at Waxham Barn on an uncommonly cold May evening a couple of years ago to raise money for the Sea Palling inshore lifeboat. Richard's turn culminated in his own distinctive version of Foggy Dew.

It was back in the sunshine of August 1991 that I got a perfect close-up of the Davies style afloat. I joined his crew on Cromer lifeboat for the start of the annual raft race. We followed an impressive flotilla of fun along the route.

Suddenly, Richard took a full-throated diversion further out. His hat flew over the side. He followed suit to retrieve it, inviting me to take the helm or join the search party as jet skiers, all noise and bravado, tested themselves against waves of the lifeboat.

I went white, sat tight and asked to go home. "Never heard of a seasick Skipper!" bellowed our man overboard, holding up his hat triumphantly.

Cromer will come to a standstill at 2pm next Wednesday (May 19) for his funeral at the parish church. We'll share a silver collection of stories about a king-sized man of the sea who could intimidate and infuriate – but never failed to invigorate.

SENIOR MOMENT

March, 2012

There's nothing like your next birthday for concentrating what's left of a grasshopper mind at my stage of life. This weekend brings what old country boys called "anuther notch on th'ole stick" as they whittled, whistled and made light of their Norfolk years.

One who refused to hand in his dinner pail until he had sniffed the prospect of reaching three figures told me age was simply a case of mind over matter ... "If yew dunt mind, bor, that dunt matter."

I suggest this little nugget of rural wisdom had been unwrapped and handed to him by another village venerable, possibly in a Victorian harvest field as a companionable evening sun glinted on sickle, scythe, beer tankards and the easy banter of reapers swishing through a golden sea of corn.

Some will insist there's nothing more responsible for the good old days than a bad memory but there can be little wrong in making the best of flimsy material when asked for a few edited highlights from the past.

I didn't have the pleasure of interviewing a Norfolk centenarian renowned for a colourfully cussed streak. It was put to him that he must have seen many big changes during his lifetime. "Yis" he spluttered, "an' I hev opposed evra flippin' one on'em!"

That's a bit extreme. Golden and diamond wedding couples I encountered as a diligent young reporter in the 1960s mixed enough home-made rhubarb wine and cosy platitudes to ensure marriage could survive the toughest of trials.

A readiness to "give and take" proved the most cited example behind a blissful union – although I often wondered who did most of the giving or less of the taking. "Never go to bed on an argument", "Don't buy what you can't afford", "Don't tell fibs if you can't keep a straight face" and "Try to get on with all the relatives" were other popular rules on the survival agenda.

I suspect a similar invitation to spill the beans today might encourage far more jaundiced responses, starting with an assertion that marriage is the alliance of two people, one of whom never remembers birthdays while the other never forgets them, and ending with a strong hint how more husbands would leave home if they knew how to pack a suitcase.

Perhaps I ought to simply offer thanks for birthdays as years trundle by rather than use them as excuses for raucous celebration bound to leave me confused and giddy. A hairy incident the other day reminded me how easy it can be to make a fool of yourself without really trying when little grey cells stop working.

"Beard trim" topped my list of forthcoming adventures as another week of self-improvement showed signs of stalling in a comfortable armchair embracing a Barbara Pym novel. I took a lengthy seafront walk and presented myself, healthy glow and all, outside the barber's shop several minutes before the start of his afternoon shift.

Surprise at not being joined by any other potential customers gradually turned to irritation as the "closed" sign continued to hold sway. A couple of acquaintances passing by on the pavement opposite sent cheerful messages of support for a one-man Wednesday vigil.

Wednesday! No wonder I stood out here on my own. This was the barber's half-day. I bristled with embarrassment, pretended to be reading window notices in the business next door and skulked away to make definite plans for a follicle-tickling Thursday.

Predictable lines featuring "half cut", "trimmed out" and "put that one in your clippings" sprouted freely among less sensitive friends when I recounted this sad episode. My wife spoilt her consoling speech by inferring I had memorable form in this department going back to fraught days behind the wheel.

Yes, I failed one of a series of driving tests in the 1980s after pulling up behind a long queue of traffic in Norwich and waiting patiently for it to move. Five tension-torn minutes later the examiner asked if I realised all these vehicles were parked. "Just testing," I replied. "No, I am, Proceed" he instructed.

The fact my latest senior moment went on for the best part of 20 minutes could be just the wake-up call required to enliven progress into another year with inevitable reminders that as soon as your cup of happiness is nearly full, someone always jogs your elbow.

I accept the older a man gets the further he had to walk to school as a boy. I know full maturity is beckoning by the time you try to straighten out wrinkles in your socks only to discover you're not wearing any. I like the idea that if each mistake you make is a new one, well, you are making some progress.

The old-style parish patriarchs, most of whom didn't appear to go in for beard trims on Wednesdays or any other day of the week, played cagey games when youngsters had the temerity to ask which milestone they were inscribing this time.

"I'm as owd as m'tongue an' a little owder 'an m'teeth" and "Owd enuff nut ter arsk tew menny parsunel questions" were stock answers when the question of numbers came up.

I will follow suit when my barber next inquires if I'm old enough to be out on my own.

SHARED BOOKING

March, 1999

It's always a pleasure to have a quiet word with Duncan Forbes about the state of professional soccer.

We shared a booking the other night. Very generous of the amiable Scot considering how he used to keep most of them to himself while fighting the Canary cause.

Along with Roy Waller, Radio Norfolk's man on the mike at Norwich City matches, we fielded all sorts of questions about women's football, foreign imports, refereeing standards, television coverage, favourite characters and Carrow Road fortunes.

I had to play a lot of moves from memory. Several seasons have passed since regular duties as scribe and summariser culminated in an inescapable feeling that I was getting too cynical, too sensitive, too honest with myself to stay close to the game.

"But it's a business now!" exclaimed old friends as shiny new cars paraded round the pitch before kick-off, ball sponsors waved to the crowd and hospitality boxes heaved with people wondering when the umpires would come out.

Me cynical? Well, if it's such good business, run by folk willing and able to learn from their predecessors' excesses and mistakes, how come so many clubs are in a financial pickle?

As we wait for Murdoch's millions to float down from Sky and seep through to the grass roots, the rich buy greed another away strip and the rest live beyond their means.

I enjoyed my little rant at a forum organised to mark the 40th birthday of the Norwich and District Sunday League. As that event coincided with the glory, and ultimately the anguish of the Canaries' epic FA Cup journey to within touching distance of Wembley Stadium, it took nifty footwork to avoid falling permanently into the nostalgia trap.

Duncan, now City's chief scout, could concentrate on other achievements after his crew-cut arrival at Carrow Road from Colchester in 1968. He helped take the club to Division One and Wembley for the first time as Ron Saunders' standard bearer, synonymous with raw meat, and then, much to the surprise of many pundits, continue to flourish under the more liberal and fanciful regime of John Bond.

Old jokes about "more bookings than Fred Pontin" afford Duncan the chance to emphasise yet again that he was never sent off in his Canary career. "I was carried off, in agony and in triumph, and served the odd suspension – but I never took an early bath at the invitation of the referee" boomed one of the most familiar voices in Norfolk.

Those stentorian tones used to rise above the din at Anfield and Old Trafford, and charm unsuspecting strangers at hotel receptions in Blackburn and Stoke. One of Duncan's favourite ploys was to convince people they had met before, picking up the conversation from where they had left off.

I was amazed how many times it worked. Several of his playing colleagues were impressed at the number of friends he had made around the country. Unlike most football club "humour", it was quirky, often funny and totally without malice.

Inevitably, I wandered off down memory lane several times during an evening made for reunions, using a sea of friendly faces as the perfect excuse. I covered local football as a young sports reporter – including Loke United's proud march to the FA Sunday Cup final – and even enjoyed a spell as manager of Norwich Sunday club Pegasus.

Duncan Forbes in typical whole-hearted action for the Canaries

SILVER LINING

August, 2010

These are heady times for Puckaterry Parva Rangers. One of the area's oldest junior soccer clubs limbered up for a new season with genuine hopes of flattening all before them in the next few months.

Fresh faces and bubbling ideas all along the touchline point to dramatic improvements on best achievements so far in their history – quarter-finalists in the Guzunder Cottage Hospital Trophy in 1927, when there was a record entry of eight clubs, and runners-up in Division Two of the Muckwash & District League at the time it was disbanded on the outbreak of war in 1939.

Now they're starting to speak confidently of employing their own silver engraver after a sporting revolution at Buskins Meadow. A new management team has taken over, setting a five-year target to "do the business" after extensive advertising in the local press.

"We'll be in senior football before England win the World Cup again, that's for sure," trumpeted player-manager Dasher Dowson, renowned for his sergeant-major approach to training and physical example on the pitch. "I wouldn't have come from Sowthistle Athletic if I didn't think this outfit had real potential."

His assistant, Silky Simpson, is a long-time advocate of allowing players full freedom of expression. He was a quicksilver inside-forward back in the old Norfolk & Suffolk League days. Dowson and Simpson refute suggestions their contrasting philosophies could cause confusion among players and friction between themselves.

"On the contrary, it is our opponents – and we fear no-one – who should do the worrying. If we don't know exactly what we're up to, surely they won't be able to read us at all," said Dowson during a brief break from a rigorous training beat.

The new committee agreed to do away with the club's oldest rule that all players and officials had to be born in the village or within a five-mile radius.

"We must bang shut the creaking door of dusty history and open new windows to let in the light of ambition and adventure," said newly-elected president, garage owner Harold Hutkin, as he paid tribute to all who had kept the club going since 1889.

New club chairman is Mr Hirst. Efforts are underway to discover his first name, or at least his initials for use in match programmes and on the new website. He lives 30 miles away and would not have been eligible for office under the old rules.

Mr Hirst takes a very keen interest in village activities. He hopes to obtain planning permission to build an estate for first-team buyers on the field behind Dunnock Loke where the Wesleyan Reform Chapel used to stand.

He has promised a "four-figure" sponsorship for the senior side with the option to renew and increase in the event of promotion or useful cup run or to pull out altogether if he fails to win planning permission.

"Hirst Comes First!" will be emblazoned across the front of club shirts. Vice chairman Rupert Crafter, who runs a demolition business locally, drew chuckles but no serious support when he offered his slogan for reserve team kit: "Crafter Comes After!"

A dug-out for the new management team, already dubbed "tigers in tandem" by local correspondent Mrs Wolstenholme, is being built and they hope to provide similar facilities for visitors at a peppercorn rent before the end of the season.

There are also plans to unveil a new clubhouse with showers, a bar, players' lounge and television room. Current changing facilities, the old railway carriage with wire netting over the windows, have been improved over the summer.

Operation Clean-Up revealed two dozen bantam eggs, three whistles left behind by referees anxious to get away, a pair of blue trousers, three and ninepence in old money and a bicycle pump in reasonable working order.

Last week's pre-season press conference was postponed because Mrs Wolstenholme had a funeral, a flower show and a puncture all on the same day. She was free yesterday to lead probing questions at Buskins Meadow when Mr Hirst sent a prepared statement about sponsorship plans for referees.

It read: "We hope to find a way of supporting all match officials on a regular and lucrative basis without risking allegations of seeking preferential treatment. Puckaterry Parva Rangers FC seek no more than a level playing field."

Dasher Dowson was asked what measures were being taken to get rid of their "bad boys" image after so many appearances before disciplinary commissions in recent seasons. He replied that they had slapped an immediate ban on drinking before and during matches, an obvious reference to the notorious Real Ale Incident of the 2001-02 campaign when six home players were breathalysed and booked before the start of the second half against Bosky Wanderers.

Mrs Wolstenholme inquired why local supporters should believe success was on the way. "Because I only back winners," said Mr Hirst in another prepared statement.

"They think its all clover..." sighed the probing correspondent.

SO FASHIONABLE

October, 2011

A friend with a neat turn of phrase but absolutely no respect for his elders and betters describes me as "about as upwardly mobile as an outing to Grimes Graves."

That's one of the oldest industrial sites in Europe, an extensive group of flint mines dating back to the late Neolithic period about 4,000 years ago. They had to make their own entertainment those days at Weeting in deepest Breckland, seven miles north-west of trendy Thetford.

Miners used antler picks to extract high quality flint. One of the mines remains open to the public although, for safety reasons, visitors are not allowed to crawl along the tunnels. It is possible to climb right down the shaft and see seven radiating galleries.

I declined a chance to descend into Norfolk's glorious past on a school field trip a few hundred terms ago. Fear of heights had been freely advertised in the gym as my scrawny frame shivered at the bottom of dangling ropes and mountainous wall bars. Now "scaredy-cat Skipper!" taunts plumbed fresh depths as I peered down a hole and went all giddy.

A small amount of self-respect was salvaged with a line designed to enhance my reputation as the class jester – "You won't catch me knapping, sir" – but rampant aversion to life's highs and lows set me apart as someone bound to struggle as well to make sense of that seam in the middle.

Ironically, Thetford witnessed a dramatic pitch for "with it" points at the start of my press reporting days as the Swinging Sixties dawned. Sadly, purple winklepickers failed to sweep Breckland bewties off their sensible feet and I've toed the line after a fashion ever since when it comes to not drawing attention to myself.

Happily, this brand of natural modesty, interpreted by too many as a blatant lack of adventure and ambition, cannot blind me to Norfolk's thrilling capacity for embracing a clear need to move with the times, to soar above metropolitan witticisms about bad roads, truculent tractors, noisy turkeys and regular inbreeding.

This fine old county has been on the cusp of seriously stylish much longer than our Suffolk counterparts. They reached a brief peak in Southwold after George Orwell's departure only to slide into decline on a bleak admission they couldn't even keep a bookshop going let alone keep the aspidistra flying.

Norfolk readily accepted some time ago that social clout is merely a posh version of a ding o' the lug. Transient celebrities and pushy newcomers are still trying to work out which one might be coming their way after dishing out predictable sermons built on wide skies, flat vowels and narrow minds.

Our growing reputation as a fashionable quarter is not based on the rising number of boutiques in Bowthorpe, catwalks in Corpusty or delicatessens in Deopham. Nor is it entirely dependent on how often television reality or talent show driftwood is spotted floating through the Burnhams, up towards the Creakes without a proper paddle.

"Noveau Norfolk" has much more to do with a puckish irreverence for all those silly excesses contaminating the Home Counties and other crammed corners where decimal currency appears to have been fully accepted along with wallpaper ranges inspired by the Dartford Tunnel and a fundamental need to board up inglenook fireplaces.

Dear old Norfolk, maintaining trust in buskins, binder twine and signposts pointing in roughly the right direction if the wind is in the east, is ready to blow away lingering cobwebs of suspicion and dust of insularity besetting the rustic scene since surprise pre-Olympics visits by pillaging Vikings and dastardly Danes. But it has to be a dual carriageway to the Promised Land.

Those who flee from the capital and its spreading tentacles must travel the same way at roughly the same speed as their provincial partners. That means an end to warring over street lighting, sparring over parish council priorities and tarring all natives with the same dripping brush.

A new kind of give-and-take can only enhance Norfolk's stand as a blossoming member of the seriously smart set. For a start, weekenders and second-homers can support public transport, make themselves available for organising jumble sales while the recession lasts and help clear away chairs and tables after austerity lunches, charity whist drives, psychic evenings, mother-and-toddler sessions and open meetings called to discuss opposition to rampant over-development and expansion of cultural links with Essex.

They should be prepared to join the waiting list for an allotment, offer themselves up for gentle ridicule at the annual village pantomime and deliberately mispronounce local place-names to confuse inquiring strangers.

Only then might it be possible to confine a certain sort of confrontation to "how it used to be before the reformation" pages of local history. The emphasis has to be on peaceful coexistence, not painful collision or parochial collusion, to set fresh standards and banish incidents like this...

A smart city motorist, believed to be a banker, pulled up at Weybourne and asked the way to Blakeney. "There's a signpost harf a mile down the rud," replied a helpful local. The motorist, in teasing mood, said he couldn't read.

"Well, that sign'll sewt yew a treat," replied the local. "There ent noffin' onnit"

SOAKING THE POOR

February, 2012

Some clever-clogs once said that if you remember the 1960s, you weren't there. Well, I do and I was. And I tell you straight, some of the "swinging" liberally applied to that decade was confined to sugar beet hooks flashing overtime across Norfolk's mud-spattered harvest.

Come to think of it, "topless" summed up those roadside piles waiting for a lift to the factory, "on the pot" referred to infants straining for indoor relief, "acid" kept the wireless accumulator going and "flour power" saluted the priceless art of producing proper Norfolk dumplings.

See, it all depends where you're standing (or sitting) at a certain time. Red Barn Hill at Beeston remains several worlds away from Carnaby Street in London, although missionaries in buskins and sensible tweed jackets have taken some fashion sense to the capital.

One of those rural trendsetters demonstrated growing awareness of a closing cultural gap nearly half-a-century ago when he cut out the headline "Make love, not war" from a magazine, stuck it in his front window and left space underneath to add: "Why not get married and do both?"

Astute social commentary to help put a pulsating era in perspective. However, I'm racing ahead of myself on the old boneshaker of destiny. Let's concentrate awhile on an age before I lost my innocence to a siren who told me football matches at Carrow Road weren't always in black and white. Five bob for a full house seemed like a fair deal.

We managed to get through a dozen cigarettes each playtime.... sweet ones from packets harbouring famous footballers and cricketers calling out for collection. Plenty of bartering on the cards when a rare item flipped into view.

We entertained each other with pure drivel in weird voices....and could blame it on the BBC, who banned "dialect voices and women" from reading the news in a 1951 edict. The Goons took a golden age of radio comedy to fresh heights of lunacy after Archie Andrews showed how a ventriloquist's dummy could fool some of the listeners all of the time.

We saved our tears for real tragedies... like the death of King George V1 at Sandringham, devastating East Coast floods, the loss of gifted footballers on a snowy Munich runway and the sight of bloated bundles of fur wasting from myxomatosis at the roadside.

We kept our cheers for proper celebrations... like end of rationing, Coronation tea party and sports, Roger Bannister breaking the four-minute mile barrier, winning back the Ashes after 20 years and George Formby completing an entire reel in the Nissen hut that was our palace of varieties without breaking down.

I could go on... but that's the trouble with grateful children of the Thrifty Fifties. They are so good at saving rich material there's scarcely room to get started on Jim Laker's 19 wickets in a Test against Australia, Stanley Matthews' inspirational role in the greatest F A Cup Final of them all and Norwich City's epic cup run which took them within sight of Wembley's twin towers.

STALWART TOM

May, 2009

The recent death of Walsingham stalwart Tom Moore reminded me how one willing soul could do so much good for an entire community.

Farmer Tom, independent of mind and generous of spirit, ploughed countless straight furrows as a district councillor, "working for people, not politics."

His amiable presence as father of the house always transcended discordant chamber music played by party rivals. Perhaps 55 years of working on the farm where he was born taught him to cherish uncluttered tunes.

I had the joy of sharing two of Tom's finest hours on his home patch, both on suitably bright Sundays when domestic delights took preference over the tourist trade.

Walsingham is subjected to the kind of pressures few others can understand as thousands of pilgrims arrive each year on waves of religious fervour. That tends to take away attention from any activities organised and enjoyed by locals.

In October, 1984 I cut a pink ribbon to open the new village hall, a result of 10 years' hard graft spearheaded by Tom. The bonus was meeting other characters soaked in local pride.

Charlie Brown, recently retired after a colourful career as Walsingham policeman with special responsibilities for visitors, told stories galore. My favourite concerned a colleague who claimed they were high church where he went "cors they burn that incest!"

Mary Smith confided she had a birthday the next day entitling her to the pension. Kath Nelson was rather shy about her charming habit of breaking into verse. I used one of her poems about the village hall project as a suitable backcloth to the opening ceremony.

Off to Tom's farmhouse for tea with a flock of his relatives and friends. He paid tribute to a band of inspirational helpers amid good natured cries of "Moore! Moore!".

My other call in the name of Walsingham togetherness came nearly four years later as the sun beat down on carnival day.

Tractors and floats waited for the off after judging and then, with Norwich Pipe Band up front, snaked through the streets to village hall and playing field – familiar territory for me.

*Tom Moore with
Walsingham's Best
Kept Village plaque
in 1977*

I accepted Tom's invitation to walk with him at the head of the parade. "We're the pilgrims today," he chortled as priests and nuns popped out to watch.

Tom Moore's impressive Norfolk innings ended as a fresh cricket season began with the gorse ablaze, bluebells congregating in secret places and rain stopping play now and again.

Neville Cardus pointed out many blossom-shakers ago: "A season does not burst on us, as football does, full grown and arrogant. It comes to us every year with a modesty that matches the slender tracery of leaf and twig, which belong to the setting of every true cricket field in the season's first days."

William Blake wrote a poem about the game. Lord Byron played for Harrow. James Joyce was an enthusiast. Samuel Beckett is the only Nobel

Prize winner for Literature to be mentioned in Wisden, the cricketers' bible.

Many other academics and literary figures, like Edmund Blunden, Siegfried Sassoon and Hugh de Selincourt, took cricket as a diversion, but one to be passionately admired.

Then there was J M Barrie, biggest inspiration for those of us for whom skill was never able to match enthusiasm. The creator of Peter Pan didn't want to grow up and his love affair with cricket never waned.

He formed a team of literary colleagues who were fond of the game but, to put it mildly, short on talent. Barrie led them frequently to resounding defeat. The more distinguished as authors were his men, the worse they played – with the notable exception of Conan Doyle.

On the train journey to their first match, Barrie tried to get across finer points of the game. Like which side of the bat you hit with. He asked two African travellers the African for "Heaven help us!" The reply was "Allahakbar!" From this his side took the name "Allahakbarries".

Of course, a few unfortunate souls will never understand the game. Abdul Aziz, also known as Abdul the Damned, was a Turkish potentate. On seeing English sailors playing cricket he exclaimed: "Remarkable! But what needless exertion! Why do you not compel your slaves and concubines to perform it for you?"

An item in the personal column of World Sport best sums up the game's charms: "Retired gentleman wishes to meet widow with two tickets for Third Test with view to matrimony.

"Kindly send photograph of tickets."

STEWKEY NEWS

September, 2011

It can be dangerous fun dipping into Norfolk's murky pronunciation waters, even for those who claim to read every current fad or ride on the surf of generally accepted local wisdom.

Prime Minister David Cameron made his own little splash when he came among us with a reminder that superfast broadband is the best thing since sliced bread – not something you spread on it.

He also made a brave stab at ingratiating himself with a holiday trade desperate for another really big celebrity endorsement. Blakeney, Brancaster, Holkham and Wells can print "Dave loves us!" stickers. The Broads may be entitled to a "Camerons are coming!" campaign. Stiffkey must wait to see if a Downing Street mention works any kind of spell.

Our leader suggested he had been pronouncing the coastal village incorrectly as it should be Stookey. Mr Cameron's "know your Norfolk" advisors were soon put in their place by a letter to this newspaper claiming that as a rule people living and working in the area still called it Stiffkey "in spite of their accents".

The crisp missive from Gerard Elston continued; "A minority of dispensable incomers are now supported by a prime minister who has been told to call it Stookey. I was born in Holkham which until recently had a pronounced L in it."

Back soon to that sandy paradise many feel we should have kept quiet about. First, a few pointers from history to indicate this Stiffkey business has been setting different tongues wagging at least since the Domesday Book recorded the place as Stuckai.

One of the parish's most illustrious sons stirred it up. Letters in the *Papers of Nathaniel Bacon of Stiffkey (1596-1602)* show spelling by locals and London correspondents as variable as Stiffkey, Styfkey, Stewkey and Stewky, suggesting two or more pronunciations were regularly in use over 400 years ago.

My good-natured inquiries among indigenous remnants in more recent times, revered characters like marshman Joe Jordan, tipped the balance firmly in favour of Stewkey being confined to labels for the renowned local cockles delicacy of Stewkey Blues.

It is deemed rather presumptuous of well-heeled newcomers, smart second-homers, passing celebrities and opportunist politicians to set any kind of pronunciation agenda.

Perhaps it's best to follow the old adage "When in Stiffkey, dew what the remaining natives dew." That is why former prime minister John Major emerges from his homely retreat a few miles along the coast to exclaim; "Cor blarst me, thass a rare noice day in Webbun!"

Back to Holkham and the Case of the Missing L. That must be down to the cream of Chelsea-on-Sea torkin proper on their missionary trips. They prefer Hewkum or Hokum (why do I so enjoy the latter?) before a day's shopping in Hewlt. Locals ignore all new rules by sticking to Halt!. Sounds like an instruction to me.

Mind you, I have heard proud natives taking the L out of Holme further along the coast and disagreeing openly over whether Cley should come out as Cly or Clay. Our younger son considered it reasonable to mock all confusion by calling it Clee whenever we passed through during his openly rebellious years.

There is a strong theory that the Barnum Markit brigade are simply exacting revenge for being lured to a county with so many pronunciation pitfalls. Yes, there are loads of Norfolk place-names designed to give locals the chance to fall about in uncontrolled mirth as newcomers and visitors tumble headlong into the same old traps.

This practice is not peculiar to Norfolk but is bound to carry extra relish in a spot where natives have been forced to put up with well-rehearsed jibes about being slow on the uptake but quick to shun all outside influences.

While there may not be too much mileage left in Wymondham, Costessey and Happisburgh – who did take the P out of that coastal gem? – faces still light up when strangers ask the way to Alburgh, Guist, Hautbois, Postwick, Skeyton, Tacolneston, Warham and Worstead. Strange abbreviations see Garboldisham reduced to Garblesham, Hunworth to Hunny, Ingoldisthorpe to Inglesthorpe and Hindolveston to Hindol. Gillingham, near Beccles, has a hard G, unlike its much larger Kent counterpart. Northrepps and Southrepps can turn into Nordrupps and Sudrupps if locals are in the mood.

Places with similar sounding names abound. For example, Booton is a small community near Reepham while Boughton is not far from Downham Market. There are several twins living some way from each other. There's one Billingford near East Dereham and another near Diss. You can find one Croxton three miles east of Fakenham and the other three miles north of Thetford.

For those arriving on the Autumn Special at Chelsea-on-Sea, a little reminder to make sure you know which Burnham you are after. Lord Nelson was born at Burnham Thorpe. There are six more close to each other – Burnham Market, Burnham Norton, Burnham Overy, Burnham Deepdale, Burnham Ulph and Burnham Westgate.

In fact, Burnham Overy is two villages, Overy Town and Overy Staithe. Norfolk choice and generosity know no bounds. That is why there have been so many pronounced changes in recent years. Even in dear old Stiffkey.

Stiffkey Churchyard

TOURIST TRAPS

September, 2008

One of my favourite yarns about Lord Nelson concerns an old Norfolk boy who went to have a look round Victory, the ship on which the great admiral perished in his hour of triumph at Trafalgar.

"That's the very spot where our hero fell" announced a rather earnest young guide, pointing to a raised plaque on the deck. "I ent surprised," exclaimed Nelson's rustic admirer. "I nearly beggared over the bloomin' thing m'self!"

A homely illustration of the way our heritage is packaged and sold in a fast-growing tourism market, turning dry dates and files of facts into rousing adventures starring colourful characters. It also helps explain why so many important historical events happened next door to a souvenir shop.

Fortunately, we have been spared too much marketing mayhem over Norfolk's most celebrated son although an outbreak of Nelsonmania to mark the 200th anniversary of his death did threaten to spill over into murky depths. Burnham Thorpe's leading role model was decked out as a teddy bear to offer "a more welcoming image of the county in that he will identify the cuddly, hospitable side that is underneath the Norfolk mentality."

Now, if we don't unravel that for each other, I can't see how it might be made available to newcomers and visitors. A Lady Hamilton doll whispering "Kiss me, Hardy" while fluttering her eyelashes and puckering crimson lips.... that might stand a chance.

Talking of female wiles, it seems we may have found a sultry successor at last to Gwyneth Paltrow, the actress who left dainty footprints on Holkham Beach and all over "Come to undiscovered Norfolk" brochures as she left *Shakespeare in Love*. (I won't do any clever lines about going from Bard to worse). Keira Knightley (which sounds like a plaintive plea from an old people's home) has scattered a few fresh bits of tinsel around Cley Marshes and Holkham Hall.

Quite what the lesser-spotted reedtrosher and much-valued estate worker make of all that cleavage and corset has yet to be revealed. But *The Duchess* can expect a regal reception from tourism bosses who know an uplifting prospect when they spy one.

Welcome to Keira Country! From mansion to marshes – take the Norfolk road to Hollywood! Steady, boy, or they'll be appointing a brand new spin doctor for the inevitable follow-up wave of celluloid sensations set in this neck of the woods. Cley Noon, a samphire eastern (our answer to the spaghetti western), is being touted already.

Of course, celebrity-spotting is an established Norfolk sport from Burnham Market to Brancaster Staithe while excitement over sightings of television drama crews has reached new peaks on and around the golden beaches of Swaffham. Welcome to Kingdom Country – where they put the accent on anything.

Well, while we wait for Betsy Trotwood to shoo away donkeys from the seafront at North Pickenham, I can reveal exclusively a number of glamorous locations and associated items bound to attract new hoards of visitors hooked on dynamic connections. Resist these, if they can:

• The tallest lamp-post in Sidestrand used regularly by Black Shuck before nocturnal rambles along clifftop paths.

• The biggest bush in the Stanford Battle Area used regularly by Private Godfrey during the filming of five episodes of Dad's Army.

- The site of the Woad Shop at Cockley Cley where Boadicea took on fresh supplies before setting out to sack a few Roman settlements.

- The allotment in Weston Longville where Parson Woodforde obtained fresh vegetables for occasional dinner parties. (Recipes available on request)

- The exposed spot on Weybourne Beach where John Major suddenly wondered out loud what the hell he was doing here in mid-winter.

- The square table used by Louis Marchesi during his early years in Norwich as a pastry cook before setting up an international movement for young men.

- The lay-by on the road to Blickling Hall where a coach drawn by headless horses and driven by Anne Boleyn calls in each year for its MOT.

- The spot on Yarmouth Beach where young David Copperfield first saw the Peggottys' pioneering efforts to solve a local affordable housing shortage.

- The trainers worn by Will Kemp on the final leg of his Morris-dancing marathon from London to Norwich in 1599.

- The oak tree at Poringland favoured by John Crome, founder and father-figure of the Norwich School of Painting. Don't touch if it's still wet.

Other parts? They're not a patch on Nelson's County!

TRENDY TEXTS

January, 2009

This texting craze is getting out of hand. Why, even local churches are cutting down on letters to sad souls passing by.

A wayside pulpit converted me instantly to deep reflection the other day with this message: "To every thing there is a season; and a time for every purpose under the heaven."

I thought of Carrow Road, Threadneedle Street, Heathrow's Third Runway and the Primrose Path to Eternal Credit before wondering whom I had to thank for such stirring sentiments. There was the answer – Eccles 3:1.

The heathen within me took charge. Something to do with the Goons of blessed memory? What about that settlement just along our coast? Or a tasty cake full of currants? Then the sun of knowledge dawned on me. It was an abbreviation.

Yes, those uplifting words come from Ecclesiastes, 21st book of the Old Testament, sandwiched between Proverbs and Song of Solomon.

Now I'm on the lookout for more enlightenment from Gen, Levi, Numb, Deut, Chron, Lam, Zeph, Mal, Eph, Col, Phil and, most appropriate of all, Rev.

We live, deliberate and pray in an age of abbreviations and this may have been a holy ploy to send backsliders in search of linguistic salvation. Even so, I hope we don't move casually from C of E to other shortened denominations like Meths, Congs and Baps.

The current mania for sending too many inconsequential messages to all and sundry via mobile phone or computer is having a serious effect on spelling and grammar. Take no notice of trendy "experts" who claim it is all part of an exciting evolution in our communications system.

It is slovenly, corrosive and downright insulting to a beautiful language.

Short cuts along the information highway lead all too often to power cuts when it comes to simple expression. Just watch television or tune in to certain radio programmes for an hour or so and you'll hear what I mean.

Never mind those hapless hordes falling over each other to be insulted and humiliated in reality (more like banality) shows where the label "celebrity" ensures maximum idiocy. News and sports programmes are littered with contributors struggling to get beyond "fantastic", "incredible", "unbelievable", "brilliant" and, my biggest bugbears, "gobsmacked" and "gutted".

Football has been lampooned so often for drowning in a sea of utter piffle it's hard to know when new depths are being plumbed by managers, players and a plethora of open-shirted pundits.

I yearn for the good old days of "over the moon", "game of two halves", "get a result" and "the boys gave 110 per cent" and the endearing habit of adding a letter at the end of a name to make it sound like playground selection time.

My soccer reporting seasons featured winners like Bondy, Browny, Briggsy and Forbsy. I believe that era ended at Carrow Road with the arrival of Drazen Muzinic in 1980.

I appreciate how some names ask to be curtailed in the name of eye-catching headlines – I struggled with golfer Peter Oosterhuis for years as a sub-editor on the EDP sports pages – but there can be cuts too far.

A recent campaign to keep fit with former Canaries Darren Huckaby and Craig Fleming spawned the notorious double-act "Hucks and Flem". I couldn't have been alone in thinking it sounded like a particularly virulent strain of Norfolk's most common ailment, suffin' gorn abowt.

At least we were spared the unwanted apostrophe lurking in the background to make it "Huck's" and so stay true to that raging roadside fashion for advertising cab's, pot's and leak's.

Of course, some abbreviations can be harmless fun. Jimmy Young signed off for hundreds of years with "BFN – Bye For Now" at the end of his wireless programme. Some of us grew up realising that ITMA stood for "It's That Man Again".

I don't want to go OTT about this but I do recall the BBC confusing me no end in more recent times with a snowstorm of memos heralding visits from HOC (Head Of Centre), HOB (Head Of Broadcasting) and other important figures.

Such ad-hoc arrangements left me hob-nobbing perfectly until someone with even funnier initials – it could have been Head Of Region (South East) – cantered on to the glad-handing stage.

A final moan about abuse of our language by people who think they are being cool. I'm tired of young ladies in offices who greet my phone request or inquiry with a squawk of "No probs!"

Sadly, in most cases, it turns out they would have been better advised to reply "No idea".

BOOKISH BANTER

A bookshop in the shadow of Lincoln Cathedral forestalls too many banal comments from customers with a list of "things to say" above the shelves.

My favourites: "Do you have a copy of Moby Dick? I don't mind who it's by." And "I don't know what it's called or who wrote it, but the girl in the television version had long dark hair."

I wanted to ask for any true book as I'm not keen on friction.

August 2000

VILLAGE 'ROMANCE'

July, 2010

A newspaper colleague of some 40 years ago constantly blended wisdom with humour to tempt me into reading between the lines. I asked him once for an alternative to the old football cliché saluting a grand team effort. Back came his instant solo: "It would be invidious to particularise."

I have borrowed that little gem many times, not least to avoid embarrassment when urged to come down firmly on one side or the other. A parish beauty contest with just two entrants springs to mind. Yes, my considered vote fell in favour of six months apiece on the social catwalk.

Fancy dress and bonny baby parades can add up to a fete worse than death when three prize-winners are required from batches of four or five candidates. A few summers back I must have set a new world record for "equal thirds" in small communities.

This spirit of compromise – I prefer to call it tact – nipped to the fore again recently when someone invited me to nominate a favourite local village. I refused to upset over 700 others in Norfolk and the Waveney Valley and simply pleaded "overwhelmingly spoilt for choice". There's room, however, for general verdicts.

Romance clings to the word "village" just as ivy and honeysuckle stay true to the old privy down the yard. The further we get away from the rural dream, forcibly removed in many cases, the more the need to pretend it still exists. Frankly, I think we ought to keep the exercise going, if only to frustrate those anticipating a pushover.

They need reminders to listen and to wonder if our rural resistance movement has the capacity to stay intact deep into the 21st century. For all the newcomers, commuters, tourists, week-enders and hand-rubbing developers, Norfolk village life is hanging on to a few of the qualities that sparked invasions in the first instance.

Let me make an important concession and warmly praise those who do contribute plenty to the place of their adoption. I accept also it is not too uncommon to find a native quite happy to receive but most reluctant to give. Even so, there are fundamental reasons why those good old Norfolk days, real or imaginary, will keep on demanding attention, especially in areas where radical changes are being pushed through in a hurry.

The need to compare grows ever stronger. Times have changed...say folk who sold up and moved to quieter Norfolk pastures when such an event was a matter of some curiosity and powers of absorption were hardly tested.

"We met them halfway and they gradually accepted us. Now there are so many newcomers we feel like strangers all over again. Trouble is, this time it'll take something quite extraordinary to bring us all together."

Coronations, Royal Weddings, Jubilees or being completely cut off by snow are comparatively rare. Village life can easily vegetate down a cul-de-sac. This happens when worst aspects of suburban existence are allowed to infiltrate once-rural parts. Blandness and apathy are the main enemies and it is dangerous to regard loneliness as something that drifts only around cities and towns.

Competitions along best-kept village lines can help keep alive the proper sort of spirit, sometimes resurrecting it and instilling a fresh sense of purpose into a community which had let itself go, becoming rather drab and dowdy.

These are the lucky ones, welding together best intentions of native and newcomer. Often it takes blatant dangers to stir them into concern over what they stand to lose. A host of once-attractive settlements only woke to the fact they were being turned into dormitories when snoring reached deafening levels.

Some parish councils know from bitter experience how often their logical and well-argued cases can be shoved aside by hard-hearted folk a few rungs up the ladder. They, in turn, will complain that even more powerful forces above dictate the pace and pattern of development in all areas.

We're on the cusp of yet another callous campaign to make small communities feel guilty for taking a stand. "Stick-in-the-mud" and "snobbish" are two of the labels waiting to be stuck on parish notice boards. Too many planners and developers will pay customary lip-service to "genuine local needs and wishes" and then carry on cramming and creaming off the most lucrative end of the market.

There are stirring exceptions, of course, and one of them stands out like a beacon in an area far more readily recognised for being posh and exclusive. The Blakeney Neighbourhood Housing Society, founded in 1946, provides affordable homes for local people in converted and refurbished cottages.

The waiting list is open to those born and brought up in Morston, Langham and Salthouse as well as in Cley, Blakeney and Wiveton. Urgently-needed first homes where seconds take up much of the menu.

I want to call it a Norfolk miracle. But it would be invidious to particularise.

WAKE-UP CALL

April, 2009

My road to Easter is clogged with customary good intentions. I've taken my annual vow to welcome a newly-painted holiday bandwagon careering over the horizon, to greet all visitors with a gracious smile and to accept the vital importance of tourism to our local economy.

Living in Cromer demands nothing less, and we've had the place pretty much to ourselves since last October when latecomers took a hint and headed for cover when wintry squalls needled in towards the end of the month.

We tucked in our sheets of self-sufficiency, hauled up the blanket of home rule and dived under the counterpane of familiarity.

Now comes a wake-up call as the first wave of trippers prepare to remind us coastal fundamentalists what fashionable watering places were really invented for by Victorian visionaries.

Trouble is it will take about 20 minutes of blocked pavements, renegade litter, moaning mothers, fed-up fathers, cheerless children, ignored grandparents, standstill traffic, unsociable dogs, ear-splitting ringtones and occasional hailstorms to blow all my good intentions into the old German Ocean.

It happens every year when I pop into town and along the balmy seafront after breakfast to put out the welcome mat on behalf of the Poppyland is Blooming Bewtiful Society. I'm flattened by the stampede rather than flattered by all the attention.

With thousands more answering a plea to take breaks closer to home while recession stalks the land, it could be hell out there before long. They'll put up a plaque in honour of my stand on Cromer Pier – "Killjoy was here".

Now I know what you're thinking. Why doesn't this miserable old toe-rag move out of the firing line? Is he some kind of weird Norfolk masochist to put up with these invasions since 1988? Will Cromer's wonderful new hospital offer free treatment to sad cases like him?

Fair points – and NHS should stand for Natives' Holiday Stress – but I do enjoy a good grouse at my age without the need to travel far.

I also have a fresh strategy to combat some of the blatant excesses characterising a "boom" season for spots like Cromer.

Yes, I gather it happens in other popular fleshpots. My spies tell me

Sheringham can get quite busy in July while parking in East Runton is a lottery at any time of the year.

Norfolk is a vast county of infinite variety. I remember that from a school outing to Grimes Graves in Breckland when I refused to go underground because I nursed ambitions to be upwardly mobile. (I couldn't spell claustrophobia.)

So it must make sense to spread our tourist load rather than continue to concentrate them on certain well-trampled places. That does not mean messing up quaintly quiet (or quietly quaint) corners waiting for the next coronation street party or millennium barn dance.

Even so, family cycling safaris to Baconsthorpe, Bessingham and Bradfield could do wonders for traffic flow through Cromer in high summer.

History on the hoof round Hanworth, Happisburgh (don't go too near the edge) and Hempstead and wildflower wanders at Sidestrand, Southrepps and Sustead must take some of the heat off the mean streets of Crabland.

Trains and bus excursions trumpeting the challenge to "get lost in North Norfolk" play an important role in my spread-the-load mission. Queues will shorten rather than tempers. A treasure trail in Trimingham has to be better than a bottleneck in Bodham.

It's worth reminding visitors who care that Poppyland was born because Cromer was packed out when journalist Clement Scott arrived on the Great Eastern Railway in August, 1883.

Flowery articles blossomed after his clifftop walk to Overstrand. Perhaps the holiday history of this part of the world would be completely different had he found lodgings in town, got bored with all the crowds and noise and returned next day to his London desk for spiritual refreshment.

We can't put the tourism genie back in the bottle – old Clem accepted that his championing of a pretty rural corner turned it into "Bungalow Land" – but we can show a dash more honesty as another campaign starts.

Too many people on one holiday parade can destroy the very attractions they claim to savour. Let's not be wheedled into silent submission by this current clamour for "record numbers" and "economic lifesavers".

Spread the message. Spread the load. There's room to spare down a different road.

I feel a gracious smile coming on.

WAR EFFORT

November, 2003

As our thoughts swirled like crispy autumn leaves round memorials large and small, I settled on a chilling wartime chapter that opened in my home village.

Old friend Ron Shaw, organising local history troops so effectively in next-door Litcham, pointed me towards a Beeston girl's tragic fate 85 years ago.

In fact, it turned out by a remarkable coincidence to be a tale of two Beestons ... the Norfolk one seven miles from Dereham and a rather larger community of the same name in Nottinghamshire.

A memorial to those who died in the Great War marks the way to the graveyard and the parish church perched on a hill outside my home parish. On that roll of honour are Alfred Barrett, Barnes Culley, Edward Dye, John Parke, George W Pyle, William Reynolds, Arthur Shinn and Harry Wyett – and Gracia Bolton, munitions worker.

A church notice board greets visitors passing through wooden gates. Look carefully to the left of the board and you'll spot a large house with three chimneys about 600 yards away. In the late 19th century this was known as New Farm, home of Edward Bolton and his family.

Grace Bolton was born on July 31, 1898 and spent her early childhood in and around the farm with her three brothers. Although her birth certificate gave her name as Grace, she was baptised Gracia Margaret in Beeston Church in May, 1904.

It is not clear how her involvement with the war effort began, but by 1918 she was working at No. 6 Shell Filling Factory in Chilwell, near Nottingham, and lodging with her aunt, Lily Hilliard at Regent Street in the town of Beeston nearby.

Lord Chetwynd set up the Chilwell factory in 1915 and it is claimed that practically every shell fired by British Artillery at the Battle of the Somme and over 50 percent of shells fired on the Western Front were filled at Chilwell.

July 1, 1918, had been very hot. Grace Bolton prepared to start her late shift at 6pm. Just over an hour later a huge explosion destroyed the mixing house and ripped apart two of the three milling buildings.

It was reported later that eight tons of TNT had exploded without warning, killing 134 workers and injuring more than 250. Grace was one of 25 women to perish and her death certificate says starkly: "Presumed killed as a result on an explosion. Deceased known to have been in work at the time and since missing."

In the frantic hours following the explosion bravery shown by hundreds of survivors and other rescue workers prompted the Parliamentary Secretary to the Ministry of Munitions to describe Chilwell as "the VC factory", a name that has stuck. Two workers were decorated for their prompt action to prevent ignition of a further 15 tons of TNT.

A government committee investigated several possible causes – a bolt had come loose and fallen into machinery; hot weather caused the powder to cake; even sabotage was considered – but all conclusions were dismissed in most quarters and just about every account gives the cause as "unknown".

The Beeston, Norfolk, and Beeston, Notts, memorials record her as Gracia Bolton, the name given at baptism. The Chilwell memorial records her as Grace Bolton, the name on her birth and death certificates.

She died just under a month short of her 20th birthday.

LACK OF GARLIC

This week a decade ago there were claims in a national newspaper that the great middle-class love affair with country life was over.

Thousands of city dwellers who moved to villages in the 1980s were abandoning their rustic retreats and returning to urban life. Rising commuting costs, falls in city house prices and disappointment with rural life were pushing growing numbers of people back to territory they had left behind.

Perhaps the most intriguing reason given for leaving Norfolk's charms for a return to London came from a woman who couldn't buy ginger or garlic at the local shop.

Of course, there have been distinct signs of that love affair being resumed in certain place. But you know what to do if there's so much pressure being exerted on your community by slick newcomers.

Bribe the shopkeeper not to stock ginger or garlic.

June 2000

WHAT IS LOCAL?

August, 2011

As a shameless Norfolkolic – and there's no known cure – I cannot help but suspect motives behind latest efforts to remind anyone who'll listen that our county doesn't want to be a boring photo-copy of anywhere else.

The word "local" is bursting back into fashion, albeit too late to save legions of traditional pubs and other facilities, especially in rural parts, where the very essence of self-sufficiency and parochial pride blossomed and blessed for so long.

To be precise, a Norfolk virtue when it comes to weighing up sentiments expressed largely by influential "movers and shakers", it is "localism" exercising the minds of those who claim to be genuinely interested in separating worthwhile wheat from choking chaff as 21st century threshing tackle gathers steam.

They hail it as an "ism" ready to pioneer a new model of planning tailored to meet Norfolk's special needs rather than to satisfy an inevitable national master plan for widespread development based on the sort of let-rip policies unleashed two decades ago by the calamitous Nicholas Ridley as leader of the Department Against the Environment.

His bleak legacy lingers on with invitations to treat "vibrant development" as "grotesque exploitation" and to take "exciting prospects" for "destructive juggernaut." No wonder many old hands at the Norfolk expansion game see this government's Localism Bill as little more than a sweetener to stop the peasants revolting.

Just because ludicrous housing targets and faceless regional assemblies behind them have been scrapped it does not mean a fresh lick of paint for our planning system can halt the inexorable march of even more ugly growth, most obviously affecting places within commuting distance of Norwich.

Who or what can possibly dress up extra urban sprawl around Hethersett, Wymondham and Attleborough as something Norfolk needs or deserves? Well, it is coming all the same to reinforce old forebodings about other areas with lovely green spaces to fill.

Saving what's left of Norfolk's precious character depends on more than tinkering with a format loaded blatantly in favour of destroying it. A daring strategy built on radical "dew diffrunt" beliefs must be an integral source of inspiration.

I have long advocated that all those seeking the honour of representing Norfolk at Westminster should reside for a minimum of five years in the constituency they want to send them there. A logical move to prevent a well-educated, well-spoken, well-meaning candidate plucked from the Surrey stockbroker belt spending valuable time trying to find out what a honeycart is, what crabpots do, why squit is a cornerstone of Norfolk culture and why the nit-nurse should return to her round of local schools.

Perhaps the same rule might be introduced to help foster a better appreciation of truly local needs among those who seek backing as parish, town, borough, district and county councillors... although care has to be taken not to nip all community ambitions in the bud.

A long shot, but Norfolk could be first to invoke the spirit of old rural district councils, abolished in 1974 as part of a reorganisation of local government and tacit acceptance that urbanisation was reaching parts we foolishly expected to remain out of harm.

I cut my reporting teeth on regular delights like Mitford and Launditch RDC as village representatives gathered at Dereham to show how they cared for their own little patches. These councils, created in 1894 to replace the earlier system of sanitary districts, held authority over such important matters as local planning, council housing, playgrounds and cemeteries.

Several "country cousins" biked or caught buses to meetings. Many fought their parish corners with no-nonsense comments coated in broad dialect. I recall one stalwart objecting vehemently to a growing amount of jargon in council minutes... "Why the hell carnt we git on wi' buildin' hooms stedda erectin' dwellins'?"

A favourite cutting turned up the other day told how rodent operatives in the Mitford and Launditch area were joining the "rat-race" for more mechanisation and efficiency in their rural occupation. I was there when recommendations were accepted to help those two rat catchers keep up with the times – on autocycles. And they were to get a rise in their travelling allowances.

Of course, this band of local government servants meeting in a market town with its own urban district council probably knew most, if not all of the folk they represented. Now, as so many settlements in the Dereham area carry that suburban dormitory pallor, it is hard to imagine such automatic familiarity.

Another possible bar to RDC revivals is an apparent belief among sections of Norfolk's modern generation that Mitford and Launditch were a popular music duo, along the lines of Simon and Garfunkel or Robson and Jerome.

Well, good luck to all those trying to unearth a vinyl copy of Blofield and Flegg's Greatest Hits on the Depwade Label. Meanwhile, those fearless private investigators, Forehoe and Henstead, comb the mean streets of Docking, Erpingham, Loddon and Walsingham.

They're searching for clues as to what "localism" really means.

SPORTING MINISTER

The recent death of Lord Howell of Aston Manor sent me searching for a personal memento of a meeting with him at Yarmouth in the mid-1960s. He was then Denis Howell, Minister for Sport, and I was a young press reporter on the prowl for a good story.

We sat on a wall in the sunshine – his famous rainmaking days as Minister for Drought were well into the future –and he answered all my questions at considerable length with great courtesy and perception.

However, my abiding memory of that interview concerns his whimsical response to a query about soccer referees. "I tried that job – and being Minister for Sport is a doddle in comparison. People still tell me I'm miles behind the play and ought to wear glasses so I don't miss the obvious. But now they offer me a sherry and cheese impaled on a stick while they do it!"

April, 1998

Where's your glasses, Ref?

WHITE KNUCKLES

October, 2010

I admit this offering may betray the odd dash of reluctance to embrace generally-accepted ways of our wondrous world. Some will find it a rant too far beyond Norfolk's "dew diffrunt" mantra. Frankly, I couldn't give a bollard after one of the most restless and revealing expeditions of my life.

It's about 450 miles from Cromer to Southampton and back, too many of them spent on mind-numbing motorways slicing through blessed plots including Suffolk, Cambridgeshire, Essex, Buckinghamshire, Surrey and Hampshire decorated with lunar-landscape roadworks.

If a beauty contest should be staged between the M11, M25 and the M3, the only reasonable outcome would be a dead heat for third place. Perhaps they're all designed to make our much-maligned A11 exude homeliness and render Norfolk one of the last refuges of common sense.

My nerves were as unsettled as the weather as we returned younger son to university studies on the eve of his 21st birthday. He travels by train whenever possible but extra gear for the final year required a packed car boot, mum's driving skills and dad's useless impression of a seasoned passenger.

White knuckles and weak jokes about civilisation teetering on the verge gave me away not far through Barton Mills. Lashing rain and the next-door lane sight of the driver of a thundering great lorry busy on his mobile phone did little to endear me to Essex and its Sunday afternoon delights.

Slowing down for a close-up of armies of men in bright outfits and hard hats underlined the true value of these clogged-up arteries at the heart of our transport system. They provide plenty of jobs with useful long-term prospects.

As soon as that stretch has been sorted out by the end of 2012, Whitehall directives, suitable funding and global warming permitting, all cones, diggers, rollers, dumpers, cranes, trucks, huts, maps and those with ever-widening responsibilities can take up a fresh challenge further along.

Then that bit tricolated up to greet 2012 will call out for a spot more TLC – Traffic's Limitless Cajoling – and so the barmy band plays on after years of rehearsals along the Forth Bridge.

I suppose you can get a degree in motorway maintenance or something allied towards keeping our nation on the move. The future looks like being trimmed with even more orange.....jackets, cones and a bright sun of employment that never sets ....and many of our sharpest young minds could be queuing up to find the most lucrative hard shoulders to lean on.

They would do well to accept how much of a tragic toll this driving force has taken on our green and pleasant land since 1958 when the Preston bypass opened as Britain's first stretch of motorway and the initial eight miles or so of the M6.

I don't have any figures to show how many cherished homes, family farms, buttercup meadows, wildlife havens, rural retreats and uplifting views have been wiped away since. However, my limited experience of these high-speed highways, plus anecdotal evidence from regular users (including several who have decamped to Norfolk for health and sanity reasons) hint strongly at an environmental price of cataclysmic proportions.

Right on cue as I returned to home comforts, a letter in the EDP made pertinent points about the ceaseless A11 dualling campaign. A woman who returned to Norfolk after living for a time in Buckinghamshire, one of those to suffer from a massive increase in traffic with inevitable environmental horrors, urged us to think more about quality of life.

"Huge economic growth", billed by too many influential figures as the panacea for all ills, especially when recession bites, must destroy most of what they claim to hold dear about Norfolk. Just look at motorway-mutilated counties not far away. There's plenty of choice.

Worship of King Car threatens to exhaust any system to stall fears of bigger queues, longer delays and shorter tempers. Glossy advertising, motor show trumpeting and ageing schoolboys showing off with expensive toys on certain television programmes feeds a religion failing markedly to give a prayer for life along the quiet track.

I suspected specimens and speeds might multiply as soon as vehicles went past too fast for me to take note of number plates at the side of our country lane in the early 1950s. We had to make our own entertainment.

Now I watch cities, towns and villages struggle to cope with a rising tide of traffic. We know the price of cars doesn't begin to pay for countless indirect costs... waste of land and energy, loss of amenities, expenses of traffic enforcement, pollution and the cost of accidents by uninsured drivers.

Leading economists tell us to stop paying subsidies to keep this endless loop turning. Meanwhile, younger son soothes dear old dad's nerves by offering to use trains for his well-deserved festive break.